The Lemonade Stand 2

MICHELLE FAUST AND THE LEMONADE LEGENDS

PUBLISHER
Lemonade Legend Publishing
Scottsdale, Arizona

"This beautifully crafted collection of stories takes you on an extraordinary journey. It is not a self-help book because you do not need help. You need only to look inside and see the treasures within you, the love that is meant to be shared, and the power of your own mind. People get intimidated by the perception of powerful people they see around them. They lose the understanding that they are as masterful as any of them. We are all ordinary people put on this earth to do extraordinary things. From my simple beginnings I have had both setbacks and much success. I have navigated through it all with humor, imagery, and learning the mastery of change. We are all blessed with the skills to make life better. These are stories that represent the virtues of determination, dreams, humor, resilience, and powerful mindsets. They also include unbelievable evilness, unfortunate acts of nature, and the painfully hard realities of relationships. But virtue always wins out. The Lemonade Stand is a treasure trove of magical and mysterious resources to build and strengthen your own spectacular virtue. Always remember there is Greatness within You." – Rita Davenport

Copyright © 2021 by Michelle Faust

All rights reserved. This book or any portion thereof may not be reproduced or used in any manner whatsoever without the express written permission of the publisher except for the use of brief quotations in a book review.

Printed in the United States of America

First Printing, 2021

Disclaimer

Unless otherwise indicated, all the names, characters, businesses, places, events, and incidents in this book are either the product of the author's imagination or used in a fictitious manner. Any resemblance to actual persons, living or dead, or actual events is purely coincidental.

DEDICATION

I dedicate this book to all the courageous and beautiful souls who share their stories, most notably my sisters and brother in The Lemonade Stand Books 1 and 2. I want to give special thanks to Carey Conley, who taught me how to focus on a vision; to Angel Tuccy, who showed me how to make the vision a reality; to Zondra Evans for encouraging me to take it to a higher level; and an exceptional shout-out of love and appreciation to two of the most important people for getting this book to where it is: Michelle DiMuria, who gives me a reason to get up every morning and make something of my day, and my beloved husband, Dean Faust, who loves and supports me, and has stood by my side every step of the way—even when I almost broke the bank pursuing my dream.

"Dedicate some of your life to others. Your dedication will not be a sacrifice. It will be an exhilarating experience because it is an intense effort applied to a meaningful end."—Dr. Thomas Dooley

Forward

My mama always said, *"Life is like a box of chocolates. You never know what you're gonna get."*—Forrest Gump (1994)

Chocolate has gotten me through some dark times in my life! Perhaps it is a reminder of goodness, much like lemonade.

For starters, the night I learned my date to the high school dance was paid to take me. Nothing like the best night of your life being shattered into a million pieces. I began to wonder why anyone would do that to another human being. **Chocolate of choice that night: Mr. Goodbar.**

The night I learned my grandfather was in hospital, back in 2002, I was so angry at the world. I had just started school at Phoenix College. I was excited to finally be pursuing my degree and then this happens. Little did I know that Friday would be the last time I would ever see him alive. Four days after he was admitted into hospital, he died. He was the one who taught me about the importance of loving yourself and how to have fun in life! **Chocolate of choice, to honor my grandfather: hot chocolate with marshmallows.**

My life changed once again in 2011. In September, my grandmother became ill. She ended up in hospital with sepsis. I was heartbroken, knowing this would be the last time I would ever see her. I sat in her room, held her hand, and thanked her for all the amazing memories. For teaching me how to crochet and teaching me to appreciate a good musical. The Sound of Music and Meet Me in St. Louis will forever be ours, Nana. She was an amazing woman who I looked up to and admired. I will cherish our memories forever. **Chocolate of choice the night my grandmother passed: a Hershey Kiss.**

Another rocky year for me was 2014 - the year my other grandfather died. I remember it like it was yesterday. We were sitting at the table, talking, and just enjoying each other's company. We were watching Despicable Me on TV, and we shared a blueberry muffin. It was one of my favorite memories. I did not know that would be our last memory together, like this. That night, my grandfather ended up in hospital. I was thankful for the time we spent together - the memories that will live on forever. **Chocolate of choice the night my grandfather died: Mexican Hot Chocolate with a side of chocolate-coated raisins.**

Whether you are grieving the loss of a loved one, escaping from an abusive relationship, overcoming trauma, or trying to make sense of it all, your mental health should be a priority in your life. Whether that means taking time for yourself and disconnecting from social media, reconnecting with your family and friends, having a self-care day, which might include binge-watching your favorite movie or TV show, or grabbing a pen and paper and writing down what you are feeling in that moment. As someone who has post-traumatic stress disorder (PTSD), I know firsthand the importance of taking care of my mental health. Every day I write down what I am thankful for. I am thankful for my BEE tribe, a group of individuals that I can count on when I feel myself falling down a rabbit hole. A place no one wants to go. Yes, I have been there, and let me tell you it's one of the worst places I have ever been. My advice to you? Seek help when you are ready, create your own tribe (big or small), find resources that are out there, and last, but not least, do not be afraid to ask for help. It does not make you weak; it makes you human. At the end of the day, we are all human beings.

Whether you have a love for chocolate or lemonade, remember you are not alone in this world. These 15 incredible individuals share a part of their story with you. Taking you on this journey, that gives you hope. Learn from the tips and the lessons shared. Know that you are the captain of Ship Destiny, and you have more power than you know. Remember, too, you have a voice - use it when you are ready. You are stronger than you think. I look forward to watching you turn your lemons into lemonade or maybe starting up a chocolate tribe. I am all in for that one.

"Sometimes we need someone to simply be there. Not to fix anything, or to do anything, but just to let us feel that we are cared for and supported." - HealthyPlace.com

Michelle DiMuria

CEO of BEE Daring Foundation

TABLE OF CONTENTS

INTRODUCTION

Everyone has a lemonade story. When you spend more than a few minutes getting to know someone, they will often share their story of their breakthrough, details about their troubled past, or an obstacle they've overcome. When you look back at your life and realize you have turned something sour into something sweet, it is a beautiful day. What makes The Lemonade Stand book so powerful, is recognizing the strength and bravery each author took to put their story into print, for all the world to see. The bravest thing you can do is share your story. The fastest way to recover and heal is to share your story with others. To create the strongest bond with others is to put that story into a collection, called The Lemonade Stand.

I got to know Michelle right after she published her first edition of the Lemonade Stand. The best seller campaign was hot off the presses and she had been diligently working with each of her authors for several months bringing their stories to life. When it was finished, none of them wanted it to end. These authors had shared some of their darkest moments of their lives, or embarrassing moments, in print. They had formed an unshakeable bond that now united them forever. That first edition of The Lemonade Stand became more than a book, it became a community of support. It became a fountain of replenishment filling their proverbial empty cups.

My cup was emptied instantly the day I was taken off the air with no warning. For more than 10 years, I was a radio host in Denver, with a daily 2-hour business talk show. I was also the host of a Christian lifestyle show that ran in the afternoon, sharing life with moms sitting in the carpool lane. On a Wednesday in March 2017, my producer brought me and my co-host into his office and muttered the phrase "We've made a change". Five minutes later, I was being escorted out of the building. The next few days were a mixture of depression and elation. I was embarrassed because my audience was aware instantly. I was scared about next steps, but at the same time, I was excited about the opportunities. Everyone around me was offering well-meaning advice of what my next steps should be. Most of that advice was to stay in broadcasting. I was repeatedly told that if I wanted to do anything at all, that I could not do it without being on-the-air. Yet, I desperately wanted to run as far away from broadcasting as I could. For too many years, the industry had sucked the life right out of me. There was no joy going into the studio. I loved being on the air and sharing life with others, but the work environment was toxic, and had been for far too long. Finally, this was my chance to escape, to start over, with something new. When I finally made the decision to leap, I went fast. Everything began to pour out of me, like water. I was finally able to spread my wings.

There were still bumps along the way, but I had freedom and purpose guiding me over them. Obstacles did not stop me, they just slowed me down a little. With this new intense feeling of bravery, I chose to travel as a public speaker, teaching authors and entrepreneurs the power of leveraging media interviews, and what I call O.P.A (Other People's Audiences) to grow their business and influence in the marketplace.

While I encourage my clients to share their stories on the radio, television, and podcasts, Michelle takes it a step further. She has created a printing platform like no other. Sure, there are publishing companies, lots of them, but Michelle does more than publish your story in a book or a magazine. The Lemonade Stand imprint stands for something bigger than publishing. The Lemonade Stand is a ripple effect pouring goodness into the world. Michelle has created a unique community, at a time when the world needs grace and love more than ever, The Lemonade Stand is the sweetest place to be.

-Angel Tuccy, Author of ABC's Exposure

CHAPTER ONE

The Alchemy of Love & Faith
By Dawn Hopkins

"God bless the broken road that led me straight to you." -Rascal Flatts

There is a beginning to every good love story, but sometimes the road to get there is winding, rough, and broken. Through it, we can understand the healing, redemptive, and transformational power of love and faith. This, my friends, is alchemy: the process of taking something ordinary and turning it into something extraordinary, sometimes in a way we cannot explain.

The symbolism of the Phoenix Rising has always resonated with me. The Phoenix is a mythological bird that cyclically regenerates or is born again from its own ashes. Associated with fire and the sun, the Phoenix obtains new life by rising from the ashes of its previous self. Some legends say it dies in a show of flames and combustion before being born anew, each time more glorious than its previous self.

As I share my story, you will see why I relate to the themes of alchemy and the Phoenix Rising.

The Beginning

I was born and raised in the Chicago suburbs. I was the baby girl with two brothers who were five and eight years older than me. By anyone's standards, we were a successful middle-class family living in a nice neighborhood. My dad was a mechanical engineer and mom worked as a teacher's aide and administrative assistant.

Our family vacations were some of my best childhood memories. My maternal grandparents lived in the Ozarks in Arkansas, while my paternal grandmother lived in Rotonda Beach, Florida in the winter and Twin Lakes, Wisconsin in the summer. We took annual road trips to see them. I also spent summers visiting my grandmother's cottage where I'd swim, boat, fish, and waterski. To this day, those memories hold a special place in my heart.

I was also blessed to have Nanie and Papa, my "adopted grandparents." They were our next-door neighbors until I was five years old and "adopted me" after we moved. Nanie never had children of her own. I spent a lot of time at their house growing up and I visited them every summer after they moved to Florida. Unfortunately, Nanie and Papa passed away when I was in college. They were my first experience of unconditional love and they helped shape me into the woman I would later become.

While I knew that my parents loved each other and their children, their marriage was often unhealthy and dysfunctional. There was a lot of conflict which sometimes escalated into domestic violence. After it was over, everything would be swept under the rug as if it never happened. In addition to being conflict-laden, love seemed to be very conditional. I felt I needed to be perfect to be seen, loved, and valued. Starting in middle school, I poured myself into academics and athletics to escape all that was happening at home and earn my parents love and attention. In high school, I was an honors student and a springboard diver on the varsity swim team. I also ran on the JV track team my freshman and sophomore year.

I absolutely loved diving. It was a wonderful outlet for me, and I was reall good at it. When my dad was in town, he would attend my diving meets and video record them. In the beginning, I loved having him there to support me at my meets. But that changed over time. I recall him replaying the videos in the family room and pausing them so he could show me what I did wrong. While I know he cared about me being the best athlete I could be, reviewing the videos with him left me feeling like I wasn't good enough to win his love or approval. By senior year, my interest in diving faded and I didn't pursue it further despite several college scholarship offers. Looking back, I felt I wasn't good enough to compete at that level. In addition, diving became a challenge for me in another way.

Like gymnastics or figure skating, diving is a very body conscious sport. As my body began to mature, I developed body image issues and an eating disorder called bulimarexia (bulimia). My eating was the one thing I thought I could control, yet ironically, it was completely out of control. I hid my disease in shame until I overcame it much later in life. I now know it is one of the reasons I became a wellness and mindful eating coach. **Through alchemy, our misery can become our ministry.**

The Broken Road

The Bible says to train children in the way they should go and when they grow older, they will not depart from it (Proverbs 22:6). For me, that played out in a negative way as I found myself in and out of unhealthy and dysfunctional romantic relationships, mirroring the patterns of my childhood, for most of my life.

I started dating boys at a young age in a desperate attempt to feel loved and valued. I fell "in love" my sophomore year with an older boy. We met when the boys and girls track teams practiced together. He was sweet, charming, funny, and he made me feel special. However, our love seemed doomed from the start. He was African American and Honduran, and interracial dating was not acceptable to my family. My parents forbid our relationship, so we hid it. My anger towards my parents and family grew, as did my eating disorder. I broke up with him that summer before he went off to college because I wasn't equipped to handle it. Just writing this still makes my heart hurt.

I met my second love my junior year of high school. He was also older and attending a nearby community college. Both of his parents were alcoholics, and he, too, experienced a lot of conflict in his home due to being raised in a dysfunctional family. Like two broken pieces, we were drawn to each other from day one, thinking somehow, we would make each other whole. After I graduated from high school, we attended different colleges a few hours apart. By the end of my freshman year, he was diagnosed with bipolar disorder and had developed alcohol issues. He was extremely jealous and became paranoid that I was cheating on him. We started getting into fights that would result in violent outbursts, sometimes directed toward me. Knowing this was unhealthy, I broke up with him. He started seeing a psychiatrist and a counselor, quit drinking, went on medication, and convinced me to take him back…until it happened again. This cycle went on for three more years. Our last argument took place on June 19, 1989. He got violent and left the house in a rage. This time, it broke me, and I tried to take my own life. By a miracle of God, he came back, called 911, and I was rushed to the hospital. The doctors gave me a blood transfusion and prepared my parents for the worst before taking me in for emergency surgery.

The Alchemy of Faith

At this time, I did not know God. I had gone through the motions of being Presbyterian when I was younger, but by the time I got to college, I had given up on God. I felt that if there was a God (and that was a big if), he certainly did not love me or want me. So, I chose to believe there wasn't one.

While I was in the operating room, I had a near death experience. As I transcended from my body, I was looking down on the doctors and nurses frantically trying to keep me alive, I felt an incredible peace come over me and I was enveloped in pure light and profound love. I wanted to tell everyone I was going to be fine. I didn't know what that meant, but I certainly wasn't afraid to die.

I woke up in a hospital bed with my parents looking over me. I had died and come back! When the surgeon returned, he looked at me and said to my parents, "Your daughter is a miracle." At that moment, I knew there was a God who loved me, and he had saved my life. I spent a month at an in-patient behavioral health center receiving extensive counseling while my body healed as well. I got out just weeks before my twenty-first birthday.

This would be my first iteration of the Phoenix Rising, and my initial experience with the alchemy of love.

After this happened, I broke up with my boyfriend and took a year off college, living with some girlfriends while I continued with regular counseling. This helped me both heal and grow stronger. The following year, I returned to college to pursue a graduate degree, having received a full scholarship.

Phoenix Rising

I met my first husband in 1991 during my first semester of grad school. He was the opposite of my last boyfriend, so I assumed that must be a good thing. We married in 1993 and ironically, we moved to the Phoenix area right after I received my MA.

I worked for an environmental consulting firm doing socioeconomic studies and public involvement work. Around this time, I also started to quietly look for a church. My husband was an atheist who thought that Christianity was for the weak, so I stayed in the closet with my faith. I was working, and he was attending school at Arizona State University, and things were not easy, but we never really talked about it. Then one day, he left out of the blue. I found out that he had been seeing an ex-girlfriend and decided to get back together with her. I felt numb, yet somehow knew it was for the best.

In an attempt to start over, I left my job and started working as a marketing assistant for a marketing company where my friend worked. I began attending East Valley Bible Church in Gilbert, Arizona with a friend and co-worker. I could feel God slowly healing my broken heart. **I dusted myself off and rose from the ashes once again—my second iteration of the Phoenix Rising.**

A few years later, I started dating my second husband while I was working as a marketing director at a technology company. He was the co-owner of a popular local bar and restaurant and was extremely charismatic. At the time, he was trying to get custody of his two children (who were three and eight years old) from their drug abusing mother. I was inexplicably drawn to him. We got engaged in 1998 and married a year later. We had problems from the beginning. Four months into our marriage, we were granted immediate emergency custody of his two children due to their mother's drug overdose and suicide attempt. Meanwhile, I continued to attend church (usually alone because he worked nights and weekends), knowing that I needed God more than ever.

Because his children suffered severe trauma, they were having emotional and behavioral problems. I loved them both dearly and it broke my heart to see them struggling, despite the negative effect it was having on our marriage. Six months after we got custody, I discovered I was pregnant with our daughter. I left my marketing job and began doing marketing consulting from home so I could manage the children and still work. Our daughter was born in September 2000 and she broke my heart wide open! I never knew I could love another human being so much.

The problems in my marriage and the challenges with my stepchildren only worsened after our daughter's birth. My husband was very immersed in his work and the lifestyle of being a bar owner, so I was left to handle the children on my own most of the time. He was gone evenings and weekends. When he was home, our routine (and discipline) went out the window. My stepchildren were out of control, and I was overwhelmed and falling apart. In September 2001, I left with my daughter to stay with a friend. Then, the terrorist attacks on September 11 happened. With the world in complete chaos, I returned home.

Things improved for a time, and my entrepreneurial spirit coupled with my passion for fitness led me to purchase a women's fitness franchise with a friend and former co-worker. Our business grew quickly, and I loved empowering women to take charge of their health and fitness. Within our first year of ownership, I discovered I was pregnant with my son. At the same time, my husband was drinking more, not coming home, and completely checked out while my stepchildren were spiraling out of control. I left again and stayed with some friends to sort things out. Once again, he pleaded with me to come home saying things would be different. I came back and things improved, but there were issues with my pregnancy. Thankfully, after a very scary touch-and-go third trimester, my son was born in July 2003. Who knew that my son would be little Phoenix Rising himself? My heart broke open yet again.

Yoga, Faith, & Healing

In 2004, an experience in a yoga class changed me and the direction of my life forever.

One day, a woman walked through the doors of my gym and invited me to attend a Christ-centered yoga class that night at a local church. I had no idea what that meant, but I found it intriguing so I went. There was worship music playing and the instructor quoted Isaiah 61:1-4, "They will rebuild the ancient ruins and restore the places long devastated; they will renew the ruined cities that have been devastated for generations." It is a verse about alchemy— beauty from ashes. I was moved to tears and was forever changed. It was unlike anything I had ever experienced, and I could not get enough! **Looking back, I now see it as both a promise and prophecy of the alchemy that was taking place in me, and the alchemy that was yet to come.**

I began attending Christ-centered yoga classes and church regularly. I even brought my husband with me which ignited some hope for our marriage and future together. Around the same time, I was introduced to the founder of the "Am I Hungry?" mindful eating program through a neighbor. She and I became fast friends, and the program helped me heal my relationship with my body and food.

In 2005, I enrolled in yoga teacher training despite having no plans to teach. I simply wanted to learn more about yoga and get closer to God. At the end of training, my teacher announced she was going on maternity leave and wouldn't be having classes for a while. I volunteered to take over her classes until she returned. This decision changed the course of my life. As a result of my healing and growing faith, I was baptized a few months later with my husband and stepdaughter.

Around the same time, I became a licensed "Am I Hungry?" mindful eating facilitator. Through yoga and mindful eating, I could feel God healing my mind and relationship with my body and food from the inside-out. My pain was being repurposed to not only help me, but to help others like me. **This was part of my alchemy and more beauty from ashes. My misery had become my ministry.**

In 2007, I started teaching Christ-centered yoga at the church where I experienced it for the first time and where I had been baptized. It was amazing to be a part of a thriving yoga ministry. I felt my faith growing and continued to have renewed hope for the future of my marriage even though the problems continued.

In 2008, the economy entered a recession while I was enrolled in a master yoga teacher training. At the time, my partner and I were trying to sell our fitness franchise as both of us were ready for a change, but we literally could not give it away. We decided to close our doors and reassign our members to other area gyms. Earlier that same year, I founded The Living Well Retreats. I began facilitating yoga and wellness retreats as well as offering private yoga classes, workshops, and other wellness programs. I was also assisting with yoga teacher training at the time. With the closing of my gym coupled with my passion for yoga, I decided to pursue this full time.

At this point, my husband was essentially "married to the bar" and the associated lifestyle. The stronger my faith and passion for ministry grew, the greater the chasm grew in my marriage, yet I knew that I was following God's plan for my life. My husband was not coming home at night and drinking heavily. My stepchildren were a mess, and both were experimenting with drugs and getting into trouble with the law. At this point, my stepdaughter had been diagnosed with borderline personality disorder and was having scary and violent episodes. The younger children were terrified and so was I. My husband and I separated, and he moved into a nearby house with the older children. It was one of the hardest years of my life, but I pressed on, following the path that was being laid out for me personally and professionally. All the while, my pain was being repurposed.

At the end of 2010 at one of my yoga retreats, I got a "nudge" to open a wellness center where people could come and experience holistic healing and Christ-centered wellness on a regular basis. I knew what it was doing for me, and I wanted to share that experience with other people. In 2011, The Center for Living Well (The Center) was born as a 501c3 nonprofit wellness and training center.

Love's Alchemy

While part of the yoga ministry at the church where I had been baptized, I developed a friendship with one of my yoga students, Bob. At the time, Bob was volunteering in children's ministry with his wife, Sandy. His best friend had brought him to my classes to help him de-stress, get some exercise, and connect more deeply with God.

In May of 2012, Sandy was diagnosed with late-stage ovarian cancer. I connected Bob to my "Cancer Club," a group of students who had cancer journeys of their own. We prayed together with Bob, and I began to minister to him and Sandy during her illness. As I got to know them both better, their strong and beautiful marriage inspired me. It blew me away how Bob cared for Sandy during her illness. I had never witnessed or experienced a love like that.

At the same time, my marriage completely unraveled. After years of counseling, a long separation, and no hope of reconciliation, my husband moved out for the last time in July 2012. I was terrified, but not broken.

I continued to minister to Bob and Sandy as her illness progressed. They, in turn, ministered to me through my divorce. Neither situation turned out as intended. My marriage ended in March of 2013 and Sandy passed away just six months later. Through it all, Bob and I stayed friends and continued to support each other.

The more I got to know him, the more I prayed for God to bring me "a guy like Bob." He was warm, sensitive, had a strong faith, loved his two girls, and loved and supported my ministry. When things were darkest for him, he received hope and encouragement on his yoga mat from me. He was caring for his youngest daughter in high school and trying to provide support for his newly married daughter who was expecting. Then, for several weeks, Bob stopped coming to yoga. His friends and I knew he needed to care for himself, so we gave him a scholarship, and he resumed taking classes while he continued healing from the death of his wife.

After my divorce, I had virtually no interest in dating and told God that if He had somebody in mind for me, **He would have to put them right in front of me.** I decided to focus on my ministry and raising my children. As a single mom that was more than enough.

In January 2014, Bob's youngest daughter had an emotional crisis. The effects of her trauma and grieving the loss of her mother had taken her to a point where she was cutting herself and suicidal. A mutual friend (and part of the Cancer Club) suggested Bob talk to me, since she knew my full story and my journey with my stepdaughter. We talked for hours, and I connected him to everyone I knew who I thought could help them. Over the ensuing weeks, we talked more and more, and then things began to change. Our conversations became friendlier, more personal, and even a little flirtatious. We started texting a lot—sharing jokes, movie lines, and song lyrics. We would talk on the phone for hours having deep conversations about love, life, and faith. Then one day, it was as if

God put a neon light over Bob's head and I started to see him differently. **He had been right in front of me all along!**

In March, I took my kids to Colorado for my daughter's volleyball tournament. Bob asked me to keep him posted on the team's progress, so we continued to text throughout. I remember my daughter teasing me about our texting as if we were teenagers dating. With those butterfly feelings in my gut, I asked her what she thought about it. She responded, "Mom, that would be so weird for you to date Mr. Bob, but I really like him!"

The night before our flight home, I got text messages from Bob's best friend and our friend from the Cancer Club. They both revealed he was in the hospital with heart attack symptoms. I immediately texted Bob without thinking and wrote, "I wish I was there." He later told me that these words struck a chord and made him realize he had feelings for me. I prayed myself to sleep and pleaded to God that Bob would be okay. And truth be told, I might have been a little angry at the prospect of Bob's children having to deal with this after losing their mother. I also recall praying, "And I think I have feelings for him, so please don't take him from me."

I woke up to text messages from Bob and our two friends stating that he was okay. He had an anxiety attack due to the culmination of all the stress he had experienced over the course of caring for Sandy, her death, and helping his daughter through her crisis. What a relief! I cried tears of joy and knew there was no doubt that I had feelings for him.

On the return flight home, I said a prayer to Sandy asking for guidance. It went something like this, "Sandy, I honor and respect you so much, and I have feelings for Bob. I want to honor your memory and what this family is going through. I am prepared to wait as long as it takes, but I really like him, and I don't know what to do. Please give me guidance and direction, and if possible, your blessing." At that point, I heard a small voice in my head telling me to talk to the two friends who I had been texting during Bob's ER visit.

The very next day, I was preparing to teach a yoga class (ironically the message of my class was beauty from ashes), and both of them walked in! The two of them had never been to a class together. But there they were! I was distracted as I taught my class, knowing that I *had* to talk to them. Given the unlikely and very coincidental circumstances, this had to be an answer to my prayer! After class, Bob's best friend went to change in the bathroom, so I talked to our Cancer Club friend first. After I told her, she said, "I knew that already. I had a vision of this. I will pray for you all." I then walked Bob's best friend out to his car and told him about my feelings and how I thought things were changing with me and Bob. I will never forget his response, "I don't see it." Those words were like a dagger to my heart! Oh no! What if Bob didn't feel the same way? What if I had just been imagining that things were changing? What if it was too soon?

I shared my concerns with my best friend and roommate who reminded me that guys don't share their feelings much and to trust what I was feeling and experiencing. I got a call from Bob's best friend and he began the conversation by stating, "Okay, I think I see it." He then shared how hard it was for him to wrap his head around this because he had been so close to Bob and Sandy as a couple.

At this point, I let things unfold as they would. After all, "If it's meant to be, it will be!"

Two short days later, Bob and I shared our feelings with one another. On the phone, I could tell where things were heading. But Bob was afraid his daughter might be listening, so we took it "offline" and started texting. "I love you." He said it first, then I did. I felt like I was going to puke! We texted back and forth until 2 am, knowing I had to teach yoga the next morning. Before we ended our conversation, Bob asked if he could come to my class the next morning. I reminded him that we were friends and that would never change even though everything had changed. I got there early to prepare, and Bob walked in. We hugged, ending in an awkward kiss. I told him, "No! Not until our first date," which was on St. Patrick's Day 2014. We had our real first kiss that night under a full moon. On June 28, 2015, I married my best friend, boyfriend, soul mate, and the love of my life. Bob is the greatest man I have ever known, and he loves God, me, and our family selflessly, unconditionally, and endlessly.

The Ultimate Alchemy

Less than a year after our wedding, my business partner decided to abandon the business, leaving me with the lease obligation and the debt for The Center. I was disappointed and scared, but in all honesty, I had allowed her to derail my original vision for the business during our partnership. This provided me the impetus and inspiration I needed to stand on my own two feet and create the business that had been in my heart all along. It took a while to dissolve The Center and restructure my business, but it was so worth it.

Today, I own and operate Inspiritus Yoga: Wholistic Wellness & Training Centers. My business is thriving with three training centers in Arizona, Michigan, and Canada. I also teach for a women's ministry for a local church. I have never been happier or felt more aligned with my purpose and passion. Bob is my greatest cheerleader and biggest supporter. I could never have done any of it without his love and support.

This is not to say that my life is perfect. In February of 2018, I was diagnosed with DCIS breast cancer. I was terrified to tell Bob especially after he lost his first wife to ovarian cancer. It was a scary time for all of us, but I had incredible support from my family and friends, as well as my yoga and faith communities. One day after taking one of my yoga classes, a dear friend (and another member of the Cancer Club) told me I needed to "love my cancer." At that moment, my fear dissolved, and I stopped being at war with my body. I am happy to report that I am now cancer-free and feeling great.

The Phoenix has risen yet again, and it was love that helped me heal.

Through love and forgiveness, I have released the past and have moved forward with a healthier relationship with my parents. I have done the same with my ex-husband and we are in a good space as well.

Bob and I have lived through the challenges of blending a family, my breast cancer journey, reinventing my business, and most recently a global pandemic. He has fully supported me every step of the way. He has taught me about unconditional love and how to have a healthy and thriving marriage. These events have only helped us grow stronger together and as a family. We fully embrace the message of Ecclesiastes 4:12, which states, "And though a man might prevail against one who is alone, two will withstand him—a threefold cord is not quickly broken." It was our promise to God and each other when we married and is represented on our braided wedding rings. More importantly, we try to live it each and every day.

Love truly is a powerful thing. It bears all things, believes all things, hopes all things, and endures all things (1 Corinthians 13:7). Love makes broken things whole. It is the ultimate alchemist that brings beauty from the ashes of our lives. These words from the poet Rumi describe this process so well.

"The Alchemy of Love"

Song by Deepak Chopa

You come to us from another world

From beyond the stars and void of space.

Transcendent, pure, of unimaginable beauty,

Bringing with You the essence of love

You transform all who are touched by you.

Mundane concerns, troubles, and sorrows dissolve in Your presence,

Bringing joy to ruler and ruled to peasant and king

You bewilder us with your grace.

All evils transform into goodness.

You are the master alchemist.

You light the fire of love in earth and sky

In heart and soul of every being.

Through your love existence and nonexistence merge.

All opposites unite.

All that is profane becomes sacred again.

About the Author

Dawn Hopkins is the Founder and President of Inspiritus Yoga: Wholistic Wellness & Training Centers, an international yoga school and wellness service provider with three training centers in Phoenix, Detroit, and Saskatoon, SK. Dawn holds B.A. and M.A. degrees from the University of Illinois Champaign-Urbana and she is a Master Yoga Instructor and Trainer, Yoga Therapist, Thai Yoga Massage and Reiki Practitioner, and Licensed Am I Hungry? Mindful Eating Facilitator.

Dawn has been helping people improve their health and wellness since 2002 when she co-purchased a women's fitness franchise. Her love of fitness led her to get certified as a personal trainer and mindful eating coach. With hard work, their franchise grew into one of the most successful in Arizona. She was awarded the Palo Verde Woman of the Year Award in 2007.

In 2004, Dawn had a profound spiritual experience in a faith-based yoga class that changed her life forever. She became a yoga instructor in 2006 and began teaching. Her love of yoga led her to receive a master certificate, and she began training instructors in 2008. Soon after, she founded The Living Well Retreats and began facilitating yoga and wellness retreats and workshops,

In 2011, she co-founded The Center for Living Well, a nonprofit yoga ministry and yoga school after receiving her certificate in yoga therapy. In 2017, she founded Inspiritus Yoga Wholistic Wellness and Training Centers. She was nominated for the MASK Unity Award in 2018 and continues to make her own education and growth a priority.

Dawn continues to operate and grow Inspiritus Yoga. She feels honored and blessed to help people find healing, growth, and transformation through various modalities of yoga, wholistic wellness programs, mindful eating, yoga teacher training, and continuing education. Since she discovered her life's calling, she hasn't worked a day in her life.

Dawn lives in Chandler, AZ with her husband. Their blended family includes three daughters, a son, and a granddaughter.

Contact Information

Web: https://www.inspiritusyoga.com/
Email: dawn@inspiritusyoga.com
Facebook: https://www.facebook.com/InspiritusYoga
YouTube: https://www.youtube.com/inspiritusyoga
Instagram: https://www.instagram.com/inspiritusyoga
Twitter: https://twitter.com/inspiritusyoga

CHAPTER TWO

Lemons to Lemonade: Discovering the Financial Cure

By Dr. Wendy Labat

Life is full of lemons. You can taste the bitterness of the lemons or turn them into lemonade. Here are some examples of the lemons in my life. Let me share with you how God used my lemons to make sweet lemonade.

What could have been a medical and financial disaster turned out to be a medical and financial blessing because of "practicing what I preach." A business strategy and a breast cancer diagnosis led to my discovery of the financial cure for breast cancer; formation of The Financial Cures LLC, creation of The Financial Cures SystemTM, and the start of my crusade to empower others to take control over their finances and acquire the proper protection to prevent financial ruin.

One illness or injury can limit or end a person's ability to earn an income. The interruption of income, continuation of personal expenses, plus mounting medical bills increases the likelihood of bankruptcy. Properly protecting your health, life, and finances can safeguard your money, prevent worry, reduce stress, and provide financial peace of mind that enables you to focus on your recovery.

The Lemons: My entrepreneurial journey began over thirty-six years ago when I started an office equipment company with zero business experience and limited financial resources. This was a time when there was no internet or social media, and the only thing you could do with a cell phone was make an expensive phone call. My clients were major corporations. To be considered for the big contracts, my company had to project the "right" image. That meant having a brick-and-mortar office, employees, inventory, and all the overhead that goes with it. If you projected anything less, your company was perceived as a mom-and-pop operation not capable of handling the big contracts. Payroll, rent, utilities, and other expenses had to be paid whether the company made money or not.

My company's sales grew faster than I could imagine, and so did my overhead. I needed increased sources of revenue to meet the needs of my growing business. Times got tough because my cash flow did not match the overhead expenses required to maintain that "right" image and fund the increase in business. I loved what I was doing and was not about to give it up because of the lack of sufficient finances.

The Lemonade: My limited financial resources forced me to think outside the box to meet my funding needs. I used creative ways to increase revenue, improve cash flow, and position my company for more growth and development. This experience taught me how to take control of my finances and make my money work for me. I negotiated with my clients to pay invoices sooner rather than later, with my vendors to give me better pricing and payment terms, and with my financial institutions to increase my lines of credit to support the growth of my business.

These moves enabled me to handle the increase in business my company acquired. I found alternative ways and developed strategies to attain the things necessary to move my business forward. The financial challenges I faced during this period made me a better and wiser entrepreneur. I was empowered to develop strategies to take advantage of opportunities that were presented and overcome any obstacles I was confronted with.

Fast forward to 2014; the Affordable Care Act mandated that everyone have healthcare coverage. I expanded my tax preparation business to include insurance products and financial services. Not wanting to be a hypocrite, I believed if I was going to sell my clients these products and services, I needed to acquire them for myself and my family. So, I purchased the products I was selling and sharpened my financial services skills. This move was made as part of a business and marketing strategy, not from a personal financial planning perspective.

The Lemons: In 2017, I was notified that the results of my semi-annual mammogram required a biopsy to test a growth that showed up on the image. A couple of days later, the biopsy was performed. I told myself that if the results were positive, I was going to do what was necessary to "nip it in the bud." The radiologist indicated that the results would be back in about three days.

On the third day, I called the radiology department only to be told that the results had to be obtained from the ordering physician. When I called my doctor's office to get the results, the receptionist informed me that I would have to schedule an appointment, which was fine with me. After being on hold for about three minutes, the office manager got on the line and told me that the doctor does not make appointments to discuss test results. Confused, I asked her how I could get my biopsy results. She said that I could come by the office and pick them up.

I immediately drove to the doctor's office. When I arrived, the receptionist handed me a sealed envelope that contained the results of my biopsy. Upon returning to my car, I opened the envelope and read the results. As soon as I saw the word "carcinoma" I knew that it meant breast cancer. At that moment, I felt a sense of peace come over me. This signaled to me that this would not be a death sentence, but it was not going to be an easy journey either.

I had no clue what to do, who to call, or where to go. I did know that I could not count on the doctor I just left who knew I had breast cancer and refused to discuss my results with me.

Before I left the parking lot of my doctor's office, I did not cry or panic but asked God to give me some direction. He directed me to call a friend of mine who was a breast cancer conqueror. I gave her a call and explained my situation to her. She gave me the number to her oncologist. I immediately called their office and explained my situation to the receptionist. She connected me to their patient advocate, who asked me to fax my results to her.

Upon arriving home, I faxed the results to the number I was given. Within minutes, I received a call from the advocate. She took my personal and insurance information but explained that they did not accept my health insurance. The advocate told me to give her a few minutes, and she would call me back. Sure enough, my phone rang a few minutes later. The patient advocate called me back with the number to a well-known Cancer Institute in my area and the name of a lady who was expecting my call.

I immediately called the number, spoke with the lady, and gave her my personal and insurance information. Miraculously, I had an appointment with an oncologist three days later. In the meantime, I did all kinds of research about breast cancer. I did not know anything about the disease other than what I had seen on TV commercials for breast cancer drugs. Nobody in my family had ever had breast cancer.

I called my friend to give her an update on my situation and asked her to tell me about her journey with breast cancer. She invited me over to her house to discuss the matter. Not only did she share her experience with me, but she also showed me the scars from her multiple botched reconstructive surgeries.

That prompted me to do even more research about the doctors, facility, various types of cancer, chemotherapy treatments, radiation therapy, mastectomy versus lumpectomy, and the reconstruction options available. I wanted to be prepared for my appointment with the oncologist so I could ask questions and make informed decisions about my course of treatment to conquer this disease.

At the appointment, my oncologist thoroughly explained the type of breast cancer my biopsy revealed. She gave me specific details about the various treatment options available to fight the disease.

Since I was diagnosed with the most aggressive form of breast cancer, I chose the most aggressive form of treatment.

My chemotherapy infusions were every three weeks for a year. I underwent five surgeries, multiple MRIs, CAT scans, mammograms, and lab tests. I took every type of medication you can imagine while battling the disease to counteract the side effects of the treatment. As a result, my body was weak and frail. I lost all the hair on my face, head, and body, along with all my fingernails and toenails. I also suffered from chemo brain and could not remember what I just said or what I was about to say.

This part of the journey had me at an all-time low, both physically and mentally. I was in the final stage of completing my doctorate degree and was scheduled to present the oral defense for my doctoral study, which was the last step necessary to finish my degree. One of my committee members was also a breast cancer conqueror. She encouraged me to stay strong and not give up. I was not about to give up because I was about to cross the finish line. I worked too hard and had come too far to let breast cancer, chemo brain, weakness, or frailty prevent me from completing this task.

The Lemonade: A few months later, I proudly walked across the stage with my family and friends in the audience, as they called my name, Dr. Wendy Labat, and presented me with one of the highest academic degrees conferred by a university. It was an emotional time as I reflected on my journey to accomplish this goal.

Later in the year, after my last chemotherapy infusion, the nurses and staff in the chemotherapy unit lined up (in a Soul Train line) for the ceremonial "ringing of the bell." I danced down the aisle approaching the bell to the song, "My Name Is Victory." When I got to the end and rang the bell, all the emotions that I subconsciously kept inside came pouring out. It was cleansing and refreshing to release everything as I successfully ended that part of the journey.

The Lemons: The financial costs of conquering breast cancer were astronomical. My chemotherapy infusions took place every three weeks for a year. The price tag was $67,000 for each visit totaling $1.139 million just for my chemotherapy treatment. Additionally, I had five surgeries, multiple CAT scans, MRIs, ultrasounds, mammograms, lab tests, and prescription medication that exceeded a cost of $300,000. Can you imagine having to pay those kinds of medical expenses in addition to your personal and business expenses while battling an aggressive form of breast cancer? The cost of treating this disease could have ruined my family and me financially.

The Lemonade: My health insurance paid all my medical bills. Plus, the supplemental coverage I purchased as part of my business strategy paid me a significant tax-free payout that allowed me to focus on my recovery without having to worry about money. Thank God I practiced what I preached and sowed the seeds of obedience and integrity. Those seeds allowed me to reap a significant financial harvest. I considered this "the financial cure" and hence, The Financial Cures LLC was born, and The Financial Cures SystemTM (TFCS) was developed.

Sharing my story allows others to see what happens when you "do the right thing, walk the talk, do what you tell others to do, and practice what you preach." Subsequently, this began my crusade to improve the financial lives of many entrepreneurs, business owners, families, and individuals across the U.S. using TFCS. My clients are empowered to formulate specific strategies to diagnose their financial health, take control over their finances, make their money work for them, acquire proper protection to prevent financial ruin, build a financial legacy, create generational wealth, enjoy financial freedom, and live the life they desire.

The Sweet Lemonade: Imagine having the financial cure that enables you to have all your medical bills paid and get a significant tax-free financial "shot in the arm," allowing you to focus on your recovery and eliminate the financial worry and concern about mounting medical bills and other expenses. I am on a crusade to share my experience and journey so others can realize the benefit of being proactive when it comes to having control over their finances and acquiring proper protection for their health, life, and finances.

Being ill, no matter the diagnosis is stressful enough without adding the worry about paying astronomical medical bills and meeting other personal expenses. I am living proof that it does not have to be that way.

Consider your own financial situation. Are you a faithful servant over your finances? Many people think getting more money will be the answer to all their problems. In reality, understanding how to manage money, no matter the amount, and making your money work for you is the real solution. If you do not efficiently manage and control what you have now, how will you manage and control more?

You cannot want a rich man's wealth and have a poor man's mentality. Your mindset and discipline require the transformation of your thinking and habits as they relate to your desired level of achievement. The objective is to plan where your money goes instead of wondering where it went.

To achieve your financial goals, you must know your current financial situation. Once you have a realistic picture, no matter how good or bad, it takes three essential elements to move forward. You must decide, commit, and take action to achieve them.

Most people keep a written record of their income and expenses but overlook their spending. Uncontrolled spending can prevent you from paying for the essential things you need, reducing/eliminating debt, building an emergency fund/cash reserves, and becoming financially free. Detailed tracking of your income, expenses, and most importantly, your spending helps you see a realistic picture of your financial situation.

Are you satisfied with your financial health? Do you understand why your finances are in the shape they are in? Do you suffer from any of these financial ailments? An anorexic income? Obese expenses and debt? A spending addiction? Lack proper protection? Insufficient financial knowledge? Poor mindset? Overweight tax liability? Hemorrhaging retirement and investment vehicles?

Contracted the global economic pandemic? Are you crippled by inaction?

Get empowered to diagnose and optimize your financial health. Develop and implement a strategy to improve your financial situation. You must start by taking a realistic look at your financial condition and finding the right prescription to cure your financial ills, whether it involves anorexic income, overweight expenses, obese debt, or a spending addiction.

My bestselling #1 New Release book, Diagnose Your Financial Health, was written to empower people to overcome the obstacles to winning the money game and achieve optimum financial health. Many professional women and entrepreneurs are responsible for the financial well-being of their families and businesses. It can be a struggle if you do not have the mindset, knowledge, and tools to take control over your finances, and make your money work for you.

You must sow the seeds of knowledge, discipline, and action to reap a harvest of wisdom, security, and results. It took a while for my body and mind to get back to a sense of normalcy. By the grace of God, I am on the other side, better and stronger than before. I received my Doctor of Business Administration degree in Entrepreneurship, and I am an award-winning entrepreneur, a bestselling author, an expert financial and business strategist, and an international speaker. This is how my lemons made extremely sweet lemonade.

About the Author

Dr. Wendy Labat, aka *The Financial Healer*, is an award-winning entrepreneur, bestselling author, strategist, and international speaker. She has her Doctor of Business Administration (DBA) degree in Entrepreneurship and over 36 years of experience as an entrepreneur. Dr. Labat is the CEO of The Financial Cures LLC, a financial strategy and business development firm. She also serves as the Founder and CEO of Ascend Foundation Inc., a 501(c)3 nonprofit organization, established to empower disadvantaged women to realize their dreams of entrepreneurship.

Dr. Labat shares the knowledge, experience, and wisdom garnered firsthand from the challenges she faced starting a business 36 years ago, with no business experience, limited financial resources, and most recently conquering breast cancer. This journey led her to develop *The Financial Cures System* TM (TFCS). She has improved the financial lives of many entrepreneurs, business owners, families, and individuals across the U.S. using TFCS. She empowers her clients to formulate specific strategies to diagnose their financial health; take control over their finances; make their money work for them; acquire proper protection to prevent financial ruin; build a financial legacy; create generational wealth;

and become financially free to live the life they desire. Dr. Labat wrote the Bestselling #1 New Release book, ***Diagnose Your Financial Health***, to get people started on their journey to optimize their financial health.

In addition to being one of the authors of *The Lemonade Stand: Book 2*, Dr. Wendy Labat has been featured in publications such as *Success Profiles Magazine, Authority Magazine, Lemonade Legend Magazine, Black Enterprise, and The Atlanta Tribune* to name a few. She is featured in the *50th Anniversary PBS American Portrait* broadcast. Additionally, Dr. Labat was inducted into the Marquis Who's Who as Top Entrepreneur/Business Owner.

Dedicated to her community, Dr. Wendy also serves on the Board of Directors of the Zion Hill Community Development Corporation, providing housing for homeless senior women and young adults. She is an active member of Zion Hill Baptist Church. Dr. Labat serves on the Community Action & Business Ministry charged to assist with Voter Registration, Healthcare Enrollment, Financial Literacy, and the 2020 Census count. During her career she has served as a Board Member for various business and civic organizations.

Contact Information

Facebook.com/DrWendyLabat;
Facebook.com/Wendy Labat;
info@thefinancialcures.com;;
LinkedIn.com/DrWendyLabat;
thefinancialcures.com

CHAPTER THREE

Phoenix: Rising from the Ashes, a Journey of Self-Discovery and Healing

By Christina Lombardo

"A healthy lifestyle is a lifelong journey, not a destination we reach and quit." —Christina Lombardo

Dear PTSD,

I hate you. That felt good to admit. I have heard that I wouldn't be who I am today without you, but I think I could have learned to love deeply, be compassionate, intuitive, more empathetic, and sympathetic without you. Without you, I could still have grace and patience. I wish I read about you and didn't have to know you intimately. For instance, I can read about why people murder and intellectually understand it even though I have never committed murder. I wish we never met.

I hate you. Your cold days. Your heart palpitations. Your panic attacks. Your 30 relentless years of insomnia. Your prolonged agitation makes it hard for me to hold down a job. Your fear of nothing and yet everything. I hate you. How you make me push others away. How I hope for healing, and yet you only slowly let it happen as you wait for me to relapse. You are a fucking nightmare I don't get to wake up from. I hate how you linger. I hate how you creep up on me when I am least expecting it. On the phone. In a store. With friends. Eating breakfast. I hate how you are like a darkness hiding in shadows I didn't know existed, only to haunt me on days when I'm feeling normal.

I hate you. I hate how hard you are to explain to others. I hate that you are invisible. I hate that you have so deeply wounded my soul, yet I look so normal on the outside. I hate that I know when you entered my spirit. You are heavy for me at age forty but were a burden I could not bear at age five. You entered in like a horror movie monster, unseen and in plain sight. You wrapped around me, right there in an Anchorage police station, in front of those sworn to protect me, and I felt your bitter claws stab through the webbing of my immature brain, deep into my soul, and you whispered to me, "You're never going to be enough. No one loves you. Fear everything."

I hate you. I hate the spell you cast over my body that no one can see—an unbearable yolk on my mind and heart. Yet, I am still expected to be normal. To suck it up. It's all in my head. And that's just it; YOU ARE ALL IN MY HEAD! You rested there for decades, unseen and unrecognized by anyone, including me. I read about you and was told you only attacked soldiers. By the time a doctor discovered you in me, you had done your damage. You messed with my cholesterol, my hormones, stole my sex drive, will, joy, my body's ability to digest food properly, ruined my guts, hindered my ability to bear children, and dampened my ability to hold onto healthy relationships.

I hate you. I have spent almost a decade tearing you away from me. Ripping away at my flesh to release you from me, and yet the scars will always be invisible. Doctors and more doctors. My thyroid was failing, migraines, phantom pain, all while hearing, "It is in your head." Thanks for that, Doc. How much do I owe you for having you tell me what I already know? I hate your apathetic incompetence.

I have slowly worked to find myself again, whoever the hell that is. You entered into me when I was too young to have a solid identity. To rip you from my soul and out of my brain, I have spent thousands of dollars on tests and more tests, supplements, blood work, hair analysis, counselors, psychologists, and more doctors.

I hate you. I revel in the glimmers of hope. When the sky turns blue again, and I see it has always been blue—the moment when the clouds are white again and don't seem grey. When the trees turn from grey to green, the wind hits my skin, and it feels like the first time I have ever felt that sensation. I close my eyes, breathe in the fresh air, hear the birds singing to an unknown audience, a glimmer of hope, a moment of serenity. Could it be I am finally free of you? I wonder if this is how everyone else wakes up and walks through a day? I open my eyes and feel you standing behind my peace with a 9mm pistol pointed at the back of my head, whispering in my ear, "You're never going to be enough. No one loves you. Fear everything."

But now I have the strength to whisper back, "I have decided how this ends, and you will not win."

The Ashes

Trauma is not always a singular event. It can also cross through a lifetime until the day the cycle is broken. I remember the day I was introduced to your rage in a small middle-class town in Washington; I was two. I was dancing in my diaper while my mom played the piano and sang. I didn't have a care in the world. But you, you had other plans. You descended on the moment like a hydrogen bomb. I watched as you walked up behind my mother with a plastic cup and, without a word, slammed it into the top of her skull.

The music stopped that day. I stood, staring as I watched the bright red blood seep from the back of her head. She began screaming, and my dad ran in bewildered at the scene. All you had to say was, "I told you to stop."

In a moment, you did what you do best: suck all the life from the room. Reveling in the pain you inflicted, the energy you consumed, you dropped the cup and walked away.

You moved through life, always seeking glory for yourself. Explosive if anyone got attention other than you, if anyone told you "No," or if somehow a moment was not focused on you. All eyes on you, or there was hell to pay. You had to control the room, and we all knew the rules. We were not allowed to breathe in a certain way around you, make certain noises, or eat in a particular way. If we did, without a word, you would strike first and occasionally explain the assault. There were nights you would come into my room and take all the covers off me, leaving me cold. You told me

I was a selfish asshole for wanting so many blankets, that I deserved to sleep with nothing but a sheet. That everyone in the house agreed with you. No one liked me.

You told me I was adopted and ate bugs as a child. You told me I was worthless. You told me that my parents didn't love me. You told me nobody liked me, and no one would care if I disappeared. I would wake up in the middle of the night to hear you tiptoeing across my bedroom floor. Your plan, always insidious, yet unknown to me. I would hold my breath and brace for impact. Would it be a fist to my face this time? A random hard object to the head? It was usually a pillow over my face. I learned to hold my breath for what felt like a minute, which was long enough to play dead so you would remove the pillow from my face and whisper in my ear, "Are you still alive?" I would whisper back, "Yes." You responded, "If you tell anyone, I'll kill you." I tried only once to tell my mother what you were doing. I was met with the impatient irritation of a tired woman, spent with a stressful healthcare job, a failing marriage, and four children. She said, "I don't want to hear it!" So, I kept the abuse to myself.

I started sleeping in odd places like on top of the shoes in my closet, the bottom of a coat closet, and on top of the vacuum in a different closet. I tried the garage but couldn't stand the thought of spiders. The most comfortable spot I found was behind the couch, but you found me there. While sleeping so soundly, you shoved the couch into my skull, smashing it between the wood frame of the couch and wall. You pulled it back just enough to release the pressure and said, "Nice try. Find a better hiding spot tomorrow."

I remember hearing people talk about God all the time. How loving and beautiful He was. My parents spent $100, money they said they didn't have, for a gold embossed Bible with a hologram of the Last Supper on the front. Why? I could not understand an invisible God who would unconditionally love people. What I grasped was the talk of the Devil. Of something that was constantly seeking to destroy you. THAT made sense to me. That was my daily life. The youngest of four, I tell people I was raised by wolves because it's easier than describing the nightmare I was reared in. The lack of food, clothing, affection, or much of anything resembling parenting. Oddly, an experience my older three siblings don't seem to share. It seemed they consumed everything, and I was left to the wind; leftover food and hand me down clothes. Often, the only meal I would eat in a day was the free lunch I got at school or dinner at a friend's house.

I prayed that just once, a Child Protective Services (CPS) worker would read my little mind, hear my internal screaming, see my pain, and remove me from the proverbial bed of nails I had been placed on. I was told never to speak when they came over. I wanted to cry at their feet and plead, "Take me away from here!" But I sat silent. Suffering. Neglected. An insomniac at age eight. I was spiraling down in tornado-like fashion into a small hole labeled 'Survival.'

I didn't stand a chance. You gave me weed to smoke at age seven. At age twelve, you gave me speed, took me to my first rave in Seattle, and my first strip club. By age fourteen, now living in New Jersey, I was fully involved in 90's New York nightlife, going to raves, nightclubs, using almost any drug I could get my hands on....and meth. I loved meth. I loved that it shut down the parts of my brain that would not shut up. For a moment, I would forget the years of abuse and neglect. For a moment, I felt a part of a whole, a bigger picture, and invincible. I wouldn't focus on my Stockholm Syndrome (when hostages or abuse victims' bond with their captors or abusers) or my desire for a savior in men, which would never come.

As much as I hated you, I wanted your approval. I wanted to be like you. You seemed strong and determined. You always seemed so focused, but deep down, the desires came from a place of discontentment. The world was yours to use and abuse as you saw fit. It was a game you swore you could master and not by being kind, gentle, or having integrity. You would win through scheming, using others, and taking down those you perceived to be a threat to your imaginary control.

Through the beatings, my hair being pulled out, the multiple attempts on my life, watching you destroy artwork, take a hammer to one brother, a baseball bat to another, and throw our mother down the stairs (to name a few things), I learned a lot from you. I learned about house music. I learned about fashion and shoes, how to pluck my eyebrows, and apply makeup. I learned most men are easy to control with sex and that many prefer stupid, weak, uneducated types. I learned to covet and hoard. I learned to stand up for myself. I learned to maneuver conversations, to lead people to conclusions of my choosing. If I wanted, I could have walked in your footsteps, a master manipulator, bending people to my will.

I chose integrity instead, something which deeply pissed you off. You resented the path I picked. I chose to be loving, humble, broken, and engaged with others out of mutual respect. To honor their space, to help people for the sake of helping and not for what they could do for me. I chose to give to the world what I was not afforded, love without strings attached. I did not want to be like you, cold and empty.

Even with that, my parents put the weight of your care on me. A mantle I accepted because I did not know boundaries; I didn't know how to say "no." I continued to internalize the emotional and verbal abuse throughout the decades. The lies you would tell others about me, which landed me homeless and broke. How you would lie so well to our family about me; they hated me and yet knew nothing about me. They cast me out as a pariah only so you could act as my savior. You could play the role of someone to rescue me, and I would thank you for your generosity. I was someone for you to call upon for favors later because, "Remember that one time, ten years ago when_____?" I began to fail under the weight of you.

I was told, "THEY ARE YOUR RESPONSIBILITY!" and I believed it. I was the only one who could tame the beast that was your mental illness. I learned to calm your mind, your wild ideations, and bring you back to a place of rest, if only for a moment.

The day came, though, when my soul snapped. I had an epiphany when I was approaching the age of forty, and I realized how lucky

I was. I was going to make it to forty! So many don't. How did I want my life to look? What did I want to accomplish? How did I want to live for the next forty years? I decided, in a moment, as you screamed at me on the phone for the last time, that I would release you. I deeply feared you. I feared what you would do next. I knew you would explode. I was supposed to be there for you forever, and what would come next, I did not know. What I did know is that I wasn't going to live another day under the weight of your crushing abuse. You would have your way. You would kill me, if by no other hand than my own. How many times had I picked up my pistol, placed it under my chin, and sobbing couldn't bring myself to pull the trigger? Killing myself would not end you. I knew that. Come what may, I had to release you, the first person of many I would draw hard boundaries with and cut out of my life.

What unfolded over the next months and years was an all-out assault on my character. The phone calls, the lies, the insane text messaging rants, and slanderous trash you put online about me. I had to remember, through everything, I chose to focus on a life of integrity. Anyone who knew me knew I wasn't the person you were describing. I reminded myself over and over why I was doing this, why these boundaries were necessary. You had threatened me for decades, then my husband and baby. The few times you had truly helped me in my life did not make up for the decades of emotional, physical, and psychological abuse.

At the end of the day, I didn't know who you were. I had seen so many faces over the years, and I did not know which one was the real you. But if I am honest, I met the Devil the day I met you. Cast in golden light and beauty, your only aim is to seek and destroy everything around you.

The Healing Journey

Peculiar enough, the darkness I witnessed throughout my life was exactly why I began to seek out healing. I had seen so much hatred and rage over the decades. I am a logical woman, though, who surmised that if the darkness was as deep as I had witnessed, then there must be light. The world ebbs and flows in balance, so there had to be good that reached the heavens if there was a darkness that went straight to the pits of hell. I began to study different religions. At age eight, I picked up that gold-embossed Bible, started in Genesis, and began reading it. At age fifteen, I picked up books on Rastafarianism, Hare Krishna, Judaism, Catholicism, Islam, Wiccan beliefs, and anything else I could find and try to wrap my head and heart around any type of light source. The books also came with seeking out people and friendships in all these areas to have my questions answered. I also felt I needed better daily guidance than what I had received, so at fifteen, I began to pour myself into reading self-help books authored by people like Anthony Robbins and Shad Helmstetter. I sought out anything in my free time, from books to cassette tapes, which pushed a positive message to counteract the daily negativity and retrain my brain.

At the age of thirty, now in Arizona, after a long winding road, through a lot of misinformation and a couple of cults, I found myself standing at the throne of the highest God, encased in light and love. Something I had only felt once before when I had overdosed at a rave in Baltimore, Maryland, when I was sixteen years old. At age thirty, I knew I had found what I was searching for. For the first time in my life, I felt an all-encompassing peace. I felt loved, not for anything I had or had not done, but just because I existed. I then started on a new journey to learn to love myself and undo all the trauma. All the messages which had been forced on me over the years by others, I would slowly learn to tear away from my battered soul, allow the wounds to heal, and build a new foundation for my soul without cracks, holes, or lies in it.

It took decades for me to be accurately diagnosed with Complex Post-Traumatic Stress Disorder (C-PTSD), so I gave myself a lot of grace in the healing process. What is the difference between C-PTSD and PTSD? C-PTSD typically onsets in childhood and is not one traumatic event, but a series of ongoing traumatic events. This wires the child's brain around trauma and can be harder to treat or recover from. PTSD is usually one or more short term traumatic events, which occur in adulthood. Part of my noticeable symptoms included high cholesterol and imbalanced hormones (the two typically go hand in hand since cholesterol is the building block to our steroid hormones). Since Western Medicine had provided zero help or answers, I decided to go to Eastern Medicine, and I went with Naturopathy. According to Oxford Languages, Naturopathy is "a system of alternative medicine based on the theory that diseases can be successfully treated or prevented without the use of drugs, by techniques such as control of diet, exercise, and massage." I saw a Naturopath who conducted six weeks of IV therapy on me. In that time, my cholesterol dropped back down to normal levels (from 225 to 165), and my hormones began to balance out. Each time a doctor seemed to reach the end of what they could do for me, I moved on. I believe everyone has an area of expertise, and I never stayed long enough with a doctor to become frustrated with the process.

After the naturopath, I saw a doctor for migraines and gut health. I saw another to balance the hypothyroidism I was facing. I saw a trauma counselor for EMDR therapy, learned yoga, meditation (the practice of deep focused breathing), the art of self-care, but spent most of my time with an online Chinese practitioner. Under the tutelage of a good friend, I was able to decipher the information. I learned about lifestyle balance, eating for my body, deeper meditation practices, red light therapy, and other modalities that helped my body release the trauma it held onto so deeply. The migraines all but disappeared, the severe stomach and gut pain disappeared, and my thyroid and hormone levels balanced back out. The most important pieces began to fall into place; namely, I began drawing boundaries in my life, learned what I like and don't like, found my voice, and learned to love myself.

Learning to love yourself is a peculiar thing. No one starts out thinking, "I hate myself." The reality is, we start out thinking we love ourselves, but as we go, we realize how little we do. As I began to learn the depths of my own self-pity and hatred, heal those wounds and fill in the emptiness with healing and love, I started to see how I had continued to let others walk all over me. I also learned about subtle types of abuse like gaslighting. Gaslighting is a subtle way someone else gets you to question your feelings or sanity. For example, let's say you tell a friend they hurt your feelings with something they said or did. Instead of apologizing, asking for forgiveness, and looking for a way to rectify the situation, they respond, "Maybe you should stop being so sensitive."

Another, not so clear example would be you and your significant other haven't had sex in six months. While you have tried everything you can think of, they have consistently rejected all your advances. You bring this to their attention, and they respond, "First of all, it's weird you even keep track. Who does that? And every time you ask, your timing is off. There is always something else going on. That's not my fault." In either example, whatever the issue, it's always your fault. Over time, this makes a person begin to question themselves and the reality they live in. I had to draw hard boundaries with others, making extremely difficult decisions to cut many people out of my life. Many of these individuals were family members. Family means everything to me, but as I learned, sometimes family must go first. They know you the best and can often do the most damage. As I did this, I freed up so much emotional and mental space I began to dream again. I began to remember what I am passionate about and what this entire journey has taught me.

The answer was clear: natural foods, supplements, and lifestyle changes had greatly shifted my body, mind, and healing process. I decided to follow the dream I had in my early 20's to become a holistic nutritionist. It incorporated everything I had learned as I walked on my journey to health and healing. Many had had similar health experiences as me, and it became clear I had walked the path I had with a purpose. I researched schools but still sat on the idea for a year. I knew what I wanted to do but doubted myself, my ability, and that anyone would listen. I first went through a program in Phoenix called Hustle PHX. They help young entrepreneurs learn the ropes of having a business for a nominal fee. I then hired a business coach who walked me through my marketing and launching my business. I truly could not have done it without her or the support of the other phenomenal women I met in that group. I was so nervous; I literally threw up before my first potential client phone call! I then decided, to separate myself from the masses, I needed to become certified (it's not required in Arizona). I looked back at those schools I had researched, picked one, put it on a credit card, and jumped in! It took six months of intense studying, and I couldn't have been more excited about the process and growth I went through and the greater help I would be able to provide my clients.

I truly walked into business as most do, knowing nothing. But I heard once if you are not growing, you're dying. So, I chose growth. I knew food, nutrition, and lifestyle, so I led with that. I have a heart for honest, loving communication, and I led with that also. I felt the first few calls and clients were absolute disasters! How else do we grow, though? Over time, I built out specific programs to help clients suffering from adrenal fatigue, hypothyroidism, PCOS, stomach and gut issues, and histamine intolerance. Each program has proven, hand-picked recipes created by me to help the body recover as quickly as possible, although this takes time. One six-week program for histamine intolerance, for example, cuts out the top inflammatory foods (wheat, sugar, corn, and soy). A histamine diet cuts out so many foods, such as fermented foods, dried fruits, and certain types of vegetables, that a person can give up before they even begin. I include recipes for breakfast, lunch, dinner, and snacks, as well as shopping lists, wellness practices, and recommended supplements. One client who suffered from a histamine intolerance followed this plan and saw an immediate reduction in hives (which may be associated with the issue). Over time, and testing out different foods, she could eat all foods again, her hives disappeared, her gut health improved, resulting in less brain fog, more energy, and better sleep. There is no magic pill or shake. The end may never seem in sight but getting our bodies back to a state of balance is absolutely possible when we give it time and are patient with ourselves. In closing, I would like to share my goodbye letter to PTSD.

Dear PTSD:

I hate you. I will always hate you. I hate you for me and for everyone who suffers from you. I have released the bitterness, anger, and rage, but I still have nothing but disdain for you. I chose to rise above you. I was told I would never get rid of you or heal from you. But I refused to let you define me. You will never be 'mine,' but something I experienced and moved past.

Instead of fighting the darkness, I embraced it. I devoured it, in turn, crushing you. Every time I sat down to meditate; I took away your power. Every time I got a goodnight's sleep and woke saying, "I love you, Christina," I removed your power. Little by little, I took the insurmountable mountain that was you and flattened you to a small hill I can now gaze over. I have learned I cannot fully embrace my light without embracing my darkness, and for that, I thank you. You taught me to bravely stare you down and ruin you.

You will never again control me. I am no longer scared of you. When you creep up on me, I can breathe, and instead of pushing you away, I pull you close until I crush the air from you. When it comes to tenacity, I will win. I now know I am enough. I am loved. I have absolutely nothing to fear.

I worked hard through blood, sweat, and tears to fully believe that I am well, I am healthy, and I am healed in mind, body, and spirit. Nothing will take that from me. Not even you. I hope you rot in hell.

Blessings,

Christina

"I have told you these things, so that in me you may have peace. In this world you will have trouble. But take heart! I have overcome the world." — John 16:33

I dedicate this to sunshine: No matter how dark a day may seem, you always have a way of reminding me that if you can rise each day, so can I.

About the Author

Christina was born in Seattle, Washington, and as a child moved all over the country. This led her to understand diversity, be empathetic, and fall in love with the different types of cuisine she was introduced to. Her career began in the Hospitality Industry at the age of 14. She spent 17 years in that industry, even acquiring a bachelor's degree in Hotel and Restaurant Management from Northern Arizona University. As much as she loved the industry, she absolutely had another calling. Through personal life events and learning to balance her own body through nutrition and wellness, she decided to take her life's trauma, conquered health problems, and experience to become a Certified Holistic Nutritionist.

Now, through personalized nutrition programs as well as six-week intensive programs, she walks with women through 4 Pillars of Wellness: lifestyle, nutrition, sleep habits and, physical fitness, in order to find their way back to themselves, balance their bodies, lose weight, discover self-love, and begin to heal mind, body, and spirit. Her personal goal to support women in their walk to a healthier lifestyle, understanding that diet is not one size fits all but that a healthy lifestyle is a lifelong journey; it is not a destination we reach and quit. Christina currently lives in Phoenix, Arizona, with her spouse and amazing son.

Contact Information

FB: www.facebook.com/christina.lombardo.35
Business FB: www.facebook.com/ForkThisbyChristina/
IG: @christinanutritionandwellness
TikTok: @christinanutrition

CHAPTER FOUR

The Power of Forgiveness
By Lisa Williams

The topic of forgiveness is a difficult one for most people. While it is tough to forgive others when you've been hurt or betrayed, it's equally as difficult to forgive ourselves. As a result of forgiving, my life is filled with power and blessings. I want the same for you. What amazing freedom you will feel when you are truly able to forgive.

I call myself an "entrebeliever" and hold the amazing role of Chief Inspiration Officer at Lisa Williams Co., a business matchmaking and wealth mentorship platform. I have always had a genuine interest in people and their life stories. This curiosity served me well in my recruiting career that I accidentally landed in about 25 years ago. First, let me take a step back and share a bit about my early life and the path that led me to start my business. I was born and raised in Alaska, an amazing place to grow up. Be sure and add it to your list if you have not been there yet! I was one of those fortunate souls with two parents that loved me fiercely and poured tremendous belief in me throughout my life. I grew up thinking I could do anything if I put my mind to it.

When I was about nine years old, my world got rocked like crazy when my parents sat me down and told me my dad was leaving and didn't know if he loved my mom anymore. That is NOT something parents usually share. Most of my friends who had parents that divorced just got the news their folks were splitting up, and that was that. The next two years changed my life forever. I watched and participated (begrudgingly as spoiled self-absorbed kids do) as my parents went through a painful and joyful journey of discovering who they each were individually, and eventually, who they wanted to be together. After a LOT of hard work on themselves, they got back together. That was the first time I remember witnessing how a relationship could change using the power of faith and forgiveness. My parents provided me with a fantastic example of what an incredible partnership a marriage could be, and their relationship continues to grow since that day long ago. They showed me how you can achieve deep love after persevering through difficult times together.

I went to University in Washington State and received a degree in psychology. I met my prince charming, Curt, at the tail end of my senior year. I married him the week after I graduated from college, and we moved to California for his job about a year later. I started job hunting and ended up at Abigail Abott, a temporary employment agency. I simply went to the first place listed in the yellow pages; yes, I am dating myself. Those were the days when you applied for a job by calling them and making an appointment or merely stopping by to fill out an application. While there, they asked me to take a typing test. I told them that would definitely not do them any good (I was rubbish at typing), but could they tell me about what THEY DID?

Two hours later I landed my first job in recruiting quite by accident.

I have always gravitated towards a coaching approach to recruiting. My specialty was IT and financial services, where I placed people over and over again in an industry where people move around about every 1-2 years. I have worked 100% commission my entire life and would have it no other way. I LOVE having no cap on my income. However, after over two decades of market ups and downs, I felt less joy in my day-to-day life of matchmaking. The politics of corporate life got more complex. I had 19 bosses in 23 years. More importantly, my clients seemed also to be asking, "Is this all I am meant to do?" I wanted to offer more than just a job to those people who seemed to be telling me they wanted "to be" something new. No one ever took the class, "What am I meant to be when I grow up?" Usually, most of us land in something quite by accident as I did. Hopefully, we find relative success and fulfillment, but rarely do we continue to pursue what we are truly MEANT to do in life.

I took the advice I had given countless others and went on a journey to find MY passion and what I would do next. I knew that I wanted flexibility, time freedom, no cap on my income, and something I could dig my teeth into and start learning again. A colleague said to me, "If you look around the room, and you are the most interesting person in the room, you are in the wrong room!" I realized it had been a long time since I had learned anything or stretched myself out of my comfort zone. It was time for action and change.

I started to say yes to a whole bunch of things as I evaluated many different industries, businesses, a few franchises and considered spiritual counseling. I went to various networking groups and started working on my self-development. There was so much amazing free content out there to absorb and learn! One of the opportunities I said yes to provided me the chance to start a business in financial education, something I had always been passionate about. I started learning something new every day. As I began dreaming about what may be next for myself and my family, I realized that what I had been searching for was not another JOB, but instead a business. I decided to hire myself!

I am going to take a detour and tell you a bit about my personal life because it plays a big part in what I am doing today. As I said, I married my prince charming when I was 22 years old, the week after I graduated from college. We got married for all the right reasons. I loved Curt fiercely! We did all the things society told us to do. We got great jobs, saved, bought our first house, and had our first son six years after we were married.

The first big challenge in my adult life. Our oldest Cameron was born twelve weeks early and weighed 2 lbs. 14 ounces. When he was born, we were told he had a 50% chance of survival but that every day, those odds increased. My faith is the biggest part of my life, and no matter what the doctors said, I knew my son would be okay. He spent eight weeks in the hospital; it was one of the most heart-wrenching times in my life. But one of the happiest days when we got to take him home one month before his actual due date! He is now twenty years old and in his third year of college. You would never know that his life started out in such a scary way. I share this as it was the first kink in what I realized later was the beginning of the end of what I believed was my "perfect" marriage.

Three years later, I found myself a single mom of a three-month-old and a three-year-old. We had tried to make our marriage work for a couple of years. We went to counseling, we had our beautiful boy Connor, but we couldn't seem to find one another again. I had this amazing example of a marriage that had hit hard times like my parents did, and I thought I had all the answers to make our marriage work. I'll share a startling statistic though. The divorce rate in families with long term NICU babies is believed to be 97%. That may have to be a topic in my next book!

I'll share something a little more personal here, but again, it's a significant part of who I am and what has brought me to the point I'm at today. Shortly after we decided to end our marriage, Curt told me he had started dating my good friend. I don't know when the relationship started, but the betrayal I felt was profound. I remember when he told me it was serious. I thought, "Oh crap, I am going to need to process and get past this if I am going to put my children's needs and happiness first. I am going to be a divorcee, good grief!" I was embarrassed, ashamed, and the first person in my whole family to divorce.

For anyone that has gone through a divorce, it is like a death. Except for the relationship/person you are mourning is still alive. If you have kids, that person will be in your life for the rest of yours, most likely. At least I hope they will be as that means so much to our children. I viscerally remember those times when I would go in my closet so the boys would not hear, and I would cry and scream at God. I was his good and faithful servant, and I did not know WHY this was happening. I did continue to believe that his plan was good for my life and that He could use ALL things for good. I did a ton of work on myself for the next few years. I found an awesome counselor and figured out what my part of our breakdown in the marriage was. It turns out I played just as big a part as my husband had.

I was only 32 years old, and I knew I wanted to get married again. I knew I had better get rid of any baggage I didn't want to bring to a new relationship! I met my current husband Paul a few years later, and I am blessed to say we have a crazy blended family that we co-parent together with my ex and my friend that he married. We both have daughters, and our girls call one another sisters. We celebrate holidays together, have family dinners, and even go on vacations together. I have these things in my life because of the power of forgiveness that God blessed me with, and the abundance I have received as a result. It took time to find this peace in our lives. It was tough, and yet it was the good kind of hard, the kind that when you make it on the other side, the blessings waiting there are more than you could have imagined. My boys have four committed parents who adore them and work together for their greater good. None of this would have been possible if not for the blessing of forgiveness.

I never expected to find myself a single mom of two little boys at age 32. I was fortunate, as I always knew how to make money, but I didn't necessarily know how to manage my money.

Living on one income is tough when you are a single parent, especially in Southern California. I started by taking a class at my church similar to Dave Ramsey's Financial Peace University. Who knew that the class I took seventeen years ago would be the foundation of starting my own business! I started by taking a serious inventory of what I had and getting clear on what I was spending. I am embarrassed to say how much Starbucks was getting every day!

I had been saving my whole life since I was offered my first 401k at eighteen, but I had to divide that in half with my ex and knew I had some major catching up to do. I got to work. I worked my tail off through the grief of my divorce. I made a lot and saved a lot.

Fifteen years later, I accumulated a personal net worth of almost $2 million. Me. Not my new husband, who I adore and makes just as big a contribution to our home as I do, but ME!

That was when I started my own company. I figured if I could do that working for someone else, imagine what I could do working for myself, creating my OWN economy! I don't share this story to brag, although I am very proud of what I accomplished. I share this because I know it is possible for others as well.

If one girl from Alaska with a psychology degree can do that, imagine what YOU can do if you set your mind to it! There is nothing more POWERFUL than a made-up mind working towards a goal.

This departure from my corporate life was another great example of the gift and abundance that forgiveness has granted me. I had been at my previous firm for almost 23 years. I was a top performer for the company, made them a lot of money, and helped many people in the process. It happened subtly at first. Accounts were removed from my portfolio that I had worked with for years and given to younger women. I will not say ageism played a role but instead I call it "experiencism." I realized this company I had poured so much of my life into was pushing me out, but I didn't understand why. I still don't totally understand what happened, but the truth that I've come to realize is God was simply closing one door and opening an eternity of others! Had that company not treated me the way they had; I never would have started down this incredible next chapter of my life. It wasn't easy, but the freedom I felt was awe inspiring when I forgave them.

Wherever you are in life if your situation is not the ideal one you pictured when you were dreaming about your future self, choose to change it today! Do it for the child in you that never lived the dreams you thought you would live. Do it for YOUR children or future children. Our kids not only SAY what we SAY, they DO what we DO. If we stop growing and learning, what does that teach our kiddos?

Do you know how many thousands of ways there are to use OPM (other people's money) and OPT (other people's time) to create a passive residual income? Corporations have been doing it since the start of time and we believe every family should learn. Opportunities are everywhere. Lisa Williams Co. is on a mission to empower, equip, and inspire one million people to hire themselves! When I entered the world of business builders and entrepreneurs, it was quite different from my corporate life. There is an overwhelming feeling of abundance and generosity in the world of entrepreneurship. It is a community genuinely interested in helping others in their pursuit to success. I took the skills I mastered in corporate America and shifted them to helping others find their true passion and business pursuit through my business matchmaking and wealth mentorship programs. Imagine what this world would be like if every family had multiple income streams?

One of my goals is serving others by getting to know their story and matching them to the role that they are meant to serve in. For some, it is volunteering, a job, or creating a business! I believe we all do better in life when we serve others and find our purpose.

We offer several programs and are continually adding more valuable content. Dream Business Launch, Wealth Minded Women, and Perfect Side Gigs takes people on a journey of what it takes to be a business builder. We explore your greater purpose, your why, strengths and fears, your relationship with money, and many other topics. We focus a lot on the mental toughness needed to have your own business. In my experience, anyone can be successful, but it's those that focus most on their mindset that wins at the highest levels. We are currently partnering with twelve business pursuits that all offer a home-based business-in-a-box that our clients evaluate and make an educated decision if that business may suit them. With our help, of course!

I love the companies I work with and purposefully selected each one. To represent their brand, I need to believe in what they offer the consumer. All the companies have a product or service that is in demand in the market and somewhat recession-proof. I am a recruiter first and foremost and always have supply and demand in my head. They are all companies from which I am currently drawing an income or benefiting from the product or service they offer. By the end of the journey, our clients will have a solid idea of what it takes to build a business. Ultimately, they may decide it's easier to be an employee. While it certainly may appear easier, in my opinion, it's just not as fun!

One of my greatest passions is financial education, and our "Journey to Financial Wellness" program is a popular one. My whole career was recruiting in the financial services industry. It's the oldest and most stuck-up industry in the world, traditionally run by the wealthy, FOR the wealthy. It also happens to be the most lucrative business in the world when the demand is at the highest and supply is at the lowest. That gets me excited as a recruiter!

At the core of every business, we represent is always financial education. Financial wellness is key to success in any business. It is essential to understand how money works, where you are today, and where your end goal is financially. Most families and business owners know little about how money works. Imagine going on a road trip and having no GPS and not even knowing where you are going! That is how most business owners get into business and how most families are running their own financial roadmap. It doesn't have to be that way.

One of the hardest things I have had to overcome in my journey to building my business is a shift in mindset from employee to business builder. I have found success in building a business is 10% skillset and 90% mindset. What has helped me most is surrounding myself with amazing mentors and learning from others who have made that brave leap to start something of their own. My goal in our Dream Big Nation podcast is to share inspiring stories of others who have found their true passion and business pursuit, what they were MEANT to do. Join us and see if our tribe would help you. I promise that if you choose to start filling your mind with stories of inspiration and fulfillment, you will be more purposeful in making sure that is the kind of life YOU are living.

I want to bring joy and passion to people's lives through the principles of business building and entrepreneurship. The pillars of our firm are faith, family, finance, and "Filanthropy". We want to put more money in the hands of good people. Imagine the lives we can change due to building a business that starts with our own families. We are striving to help people become "six figure givers" as well as "six figure earners." We must generate to be generous though!

The "why" behind my shift is simple. I wasn't living up to my full potential, and I realized I was capable of doing much more. I have been through challenging adversity in my life, as we all have, and have been blessed to witness firsthand how God has used that adversity for my ultimate good. I know I was meant to use my gifts to help others discover theirs and continue to grow in my life. I have a passion for helping others find the true gifts God blessed them with and to start dreaming again. What better way to help a family than to share with them a business opportunity that will help them help themselves? To become your OWN stimulus check!

I dedicated my firm to the memory of my mom, Sue Wiese, and one of my dearest friends, Elizabeth Meier. In the span of ten months, we lost them both to horrible battles with cancer. These were two of the most inspiring and God loving women on the planet. They lived their lives with purpose, had hearts for serving, and were lifelong learners until the day they went to heaven.

Mom had a horrible brain tumor, GBM and unfortunately impacted the area of her brain that controls her speech. This was one of the more difficult parts of my mom's illness. We called mom an "over communicator". Mom had this amazing way of making everyone feel as though she was their best friend. She loved talking about all things and was an equally fabulous listener. She found it increasingly difficult to speak during the last days of her battle, but this one day, she had a moment of absolute clarity. We were lying on her bed, side by side, and she looked me in the eye and said, "I'm ready for heaven, what a good life I have had. I have no regrets." Wow. I won't know until I am up there in heaven with them why mom and Elizabeth are no longer with us, but I am going to make sure that I live the rest of my life with intention, purpose, and discovery. And I will continue to forgive and watch how God blesses my life!

We have all experienced times when we have done wrong and have been wronged. We have sought forgiveness and given it to others. Sometimes the person we need to forgive the most is ourselves. If you haven't forgiven certain events or people, don't wait. They will be revealed when you seek God's wisdom. Journal, pray, and release those things.

"Be kind and compassionate to one another, forgiving each other, just as Christ God forgave you." -Ephesians 4:32

Bless you all in this amazing life journey, and I hope to meet you someday soon!

About the Author

Lisa Williams is an Entrebeliever, Wealth mentor, and Chief Inspiration Officer at Lisa Williams Co, creator of the Perfect Side Gigs program. After spending 25 years in a corporate career that blessed her life with financial freedom and reaching a net worth of nearly $2 million, Lisa's goal is to empower, equip and inspire 1 million to hire themselves! Perfect Side Gigs' coaching and business pursuit platform helps those interested in pursuing the path of business builder and entrepreneur, equips people with the tools necessary to make the shift and provides a variety of vetted business platforms to consider.

Lisa has been blessed with a successful recruiting career for over 27 years. She's always gravitated towards a coaching approach to recruiting and after nearly 3 decades of market ups and downs, found her learning curve had waned and that she was feeling less joy in her day-to-day life of match making. The politics of corporate life got more complex. The clients she was working with seemed to also be asking, "is this all I am meant to do?" She wanted to offer more than just a job.

Lisa decided to take the advice she had given countless others and went on a journey to find HER passion and what she would do next in life. Through that journey Lisa entered the world of business builders and entrepreneurs. Lisa has taken the skills she mastered in corporate America and has shifted to helping others find their true passion and business pursuit.

Lisa's passion is financial education, and that topic and business will always be at the core of everything she teaches. Financial wellness is key to success in any business. It also happens to be the most lucrative business in the world in a time where the demand is at the highest and supply is at the lowest.

One a personal note, Lisa is an Alaska girl born and raised, married with three kids, is a life-long learner, loves to travel, and sings in a praise band. Those that know Lisa remember a time she helped them and would agree that Lisa's faith is the biggest part of her life. One of her "whys" is that her children will never have an employee mindset, will be life-long learners and continue to find the next version of themselves.

The mission at Lisa Williams Co is to bring joy and passion to people's lives through the principles of business building and entrepreneurship. The pillars of her company are faith, family, finance and "Filanthropy"!

The "why" behind Lisa's own shift is simple. She was living life less than she knew she was capable of living. She was meant to use her gifts to help others discover theirs.

The firm is dedicated to the memory of Lisa's mom Sue Wiese and her dearest friend Elizabeth Meier.

She lost both of them to a horrible battle to cancer in the span of 10 months. These were two of the most inspiring and God loving women on the planet. They lived their lives with purpose, a heart for serving others and were lifelong learners until the day they went to heaven.

From Lisa: *"I won't know until I am up there with them why they are no longer with us, but I will make sure that I live the rest of my life with intention, purpose and discovery. I will grow into the women I was meant to become, and my prayer is that our company can help others do the same! Save some extra-dry Cooks champagne for me girls!"*

Contact Information

lisa@lisawilliamsco.com or text at 714-396-0193. Our email sometimes gets a little drowned! Please follow us on all our socials as well.

CHAPTER FIVE

A Mother's Plea
By Julie Jones

Everyone has lemons in their life that they have an opportunity to squeeze into sweet lemonade. My lemon was something I first saw as imperfections in my daughters in the form of a genetic hearing loss. I started out so devastated, lost, and hopeless. Through my faith in God, I conquered something I once believed was impossible.

I planned on having children for as long as I can remember. My family was always especially important to me. Growing up I spent time with my great-grandparents and grandparents. I even knew one of my great-great-grandmother for a short time. I saw how generations worked and wanted to start my own family one day.

When that day came, and I was pregnant, my husband, Scott, and I were so happy to be having our first child. I wanted everything to be alright. I knew our baby could hear, because I noticed she moved a lot when I was in the car with the radio on or when we sang in church. I love this as Scott and I both enjoy music.

Scott's parents were visiting from out of state, and my mother-in-law just made a nice Italian dinner when my water broke. When we got to the hospital, my doctor informed me my baby was breech, and I needed a cesarean section. I trusted him and was pretty mellow as the anesthesiologist talked me through the surgery. Not long after our beautiful and healthy daughter Ashley was born. This was one of the best moments of our lives. Scott and I both thought her precious little face resembled my dad.

I quit working right before Ashley was born so I could stay home with her. I followed all the milestones of what should happen when. The doctor told me that since she was babbling, she could hear herself talking. I could tell that she could see. Ashley was such a cute and adorable baby. I loved her so much and could not imagine my life without her. Taking care of her brought me so much joy. She was such a blessing.

I then understood God's unconditional love for us. I saw her from a perspective of how He must see us. We are His children.

What's Wrong with My Baby?

Jesus looked at them and said, "With man this is impossible, but with God all things are possible." Matthew 19:26

When Ashley turned one, I noticed that she wasn't talking like other children her age. Her peers were pointing to things and saying what they were. Being a new mom, I really didn't know what to expect when it came to speech. I knew babies did things in their own time.

I felt like I was being a bad mom or something. It hurt to hear other babies talking, and not mine. I was frustrated not knowing why. When Scott and I talked to her, she ignored us. We wondered if she was just concentrating on her toys.

I did not believe she had a hearing loss because of what the pediatrician said about her babbling. Her head would turn when motorcycles and airplanes went by. I believed if she could hear one thing, she could hear everything. Besides, Scott and I didn't have a hearing loss.

Ashley was throwing temper tantrums at age one that would typically happen during the "terrible two" stage. We were in the church parking lot one day when she laid herself down on the asphalt as she tried to bang her head up and down. I immediately put my hands underneath her head, so she didn't get hurt. I had never seen such a thing.

Finally, we were referred to an Ear, Nose, and Throat doctor to find out what was going on. She had a mild hearing loss, and I was told to bring her back in a month for another test. Was it something as simple as a cold coming on? Right before her appointment, Ashley got sick, so I had to reschedule. As the doctor did not stress any urgency, I rescheduled for a month later as I was very pregnant with our second child.

At Ashley's next ENT appointment, the doctor acknowledged Ashley still had a hearing loss and needed further testing. Those tests revealed Ashley needed hearing aids. That gave me hope, but then she shared that Ashley will eventually be deaf. My heart felt like someone just put a knife through it. I was devastated.

During my pregnancy, I wanted a healthy child. I ate better and stopped drinking soda. None of that was easy. I did everything right. I did not smoke, drink, or do drugs. I needed to understand why it was happening. Someone told me that God gave me that situation, because He knew I would do what was right by Ashley. I was thinking, "Gee, thanks God, this wasn't my plan."

I felt so hopeless. I didn't know anything about hearing loss. How was I supposed to help her? I felt like such an idiot. I had been walking around happy not knowing that the floor was going to fall right out from underneath me. As I lay curled up in my bed, I wanted to run away from the pain. I felt so empty inside. I never dreamed that was ever a possibility. I was grieving the loss of her hearing. I was mourning something she was being denied, a life like others.

If I could have talked to the hearing loss, I would have shouted, "Did you enjoy the anticipation of me being shattered while you were slowly destroying her hearing? Did you like that we were clueless? You knew all along what you were going to do to our lives being in her DNA didn't you? You were a silent sneaky little thing just lurking in the shadows. My plans did not include you. You broke my heart and stole my dreams. Thank you very much! I wish I could squish you like a bug. Why my child? It is so unfair! I hate what you have done. Ashley doesn't deserve this. I have news for you, God is on my side. My love for God is stronger than my hate for you. You will not win!"

My Faith

I can do all things through Him who strengthens me - Philippians 4:13

As a Christian, I pulled out my Bible. I read the above verse and took it to heart. It made all the difference in the world.

I had accepted Jesus into my heart at the age of seven which was good timing since that next year my parents got a divorce. I always felt like I grew up at a young age. That just made me have grit.   I believed that God had always been with me guiding my way and watching over me, but I don't think I really prayed much or thought I needed to.

Soon after my meltdown, and pulling out my Bible, I joined a Bible study at my church. The Bible became clearer and more alive. I knew the Bible was God's word, but I did not really read it other than verses at church or church camp when I was a kid. Although my husband and I went to church together since we were engaged, I felt I hadn't grown as a Christian until doing the Bible study. I soon realized God wanted a relationship with us. I was getting up at 5 a.m. some mornings to read it. I was hungry for God's word. It filled my cup.

Feeling Blessed

Right before Ashley's second ENT appointment, we had another precious and healthy girl, Heather. The nurse mentioned they did a hearing test and she passed. I didn't remember anyone mentioning a hearing test when Ashley was born.

When I got home from the hospital, I held Heather in one arm, and Ashley in the other. I felt like my life was complete. I could not have been happier. I loved them so much.

A Whole New World

Be strong! Be courageous! Do not be afraid! For the Lord your God will be with you. He will neither fail you nor forsake you. Deuteronomy 31:6.

Since Ashley had a mild to moderate hearing loss, she wasn't hearing speech. This explained why she was not talking. If you can't hear speech, you don't know how to talk. She couldn't just say, "Hey Mom, I can't hear." It's different than when an adult loses some hearing because they already know how to talk.

Ashley got hearing aids but kept pulling them out. I had this unrealistic expectation that they would be the answer to everything, and she would suddenly start hearing and talking. What was I thinking? I had to remind myself that she was only two years old. I was thankful to have had Scott's help with the hearing aids.

She ran from me when I tried to put the hearing aids on her. I waited for her to hear better and speak words, but she wasn't cooperating. I had been told not to give up and that it would take time. Wearing them for one hour a day was a good start.

I had pamphlets to review hearing loss organizations in our state. I ended up choosing a free service where a professional would come to the house for an hour once a week. That sounded great since I had a baby and a toddler. While we received a lot of great information, she told me that one hour a week was not going to be enough help for Ashley.

There were many different methodologies on how to approach hearing loss and I found it confusing. It depended on who you talked to. There was sign language, total communication a combination of sign language and other communication, or auditory verbal/oral communication.

I decided to observe different places to help determine the best option for Ashley. At one place, the kids had different disabilities which I didn't feel would be a good fit for Ashley because they weren't focusing on hearing loss. When I talked to another mom with a two-year-old who couldn't talk, I felt better finally finding someone who understood how I felt.

There was a school for the deaf, but they only used sign language. Since I grew up in the hearing world, I really didn't like that option. All I kept thinking about was that Ashley wouldn't even be able to order a cheeseburger at McDonald's one day because the cashier wouldn't know sign language. How was my child going to communicate with the world?

I wanted to find out anything I could. I went to the video store to get a movie about a boy with a hearing loss. I found it on the shelf, but another lady was trying to grab it at the same time as me. I did something I normally would not do. I aggressively grabbed it. With tears in my eyes, I told her I was sorry, but I really needed it because my child had a hearing loss.

You've Got to Have Hope

Trust in the Lord with all your heart and lean not on your own understanding; in all ways submit to Him, and He will make your paths straight. Proverbs 3:5-6

I had one more place to observe on my list, a school in Atlanta. Ashley, Heather, and I went into a little observation room with a two-way mirror. I could not believe my eyes. There were several children Ashley's age sitting with their teacher looking at a huge calendar discussing the days of the week. Those kids had a hearing loss too and were talking! I cried tears of joy. I just knew that was where my child needed to be.

The school's focus was listening and spoken language. They didn't use sign language because they believed that if you use your eyes to see what someone is doing with their hands; you aren't using your ears. This school would teach Ashley how to use her ears with hearing aids, and how to talk. They also offered speech therapy.

I couldn't believe this place existed. Ashley could learn to communicate and be part of the hearing world. Suddenly, I had so much more hope for her success in life.

The teacher asked me if my younger daughter Heather could hear. I told her about how she passed the newborn hearing test and startled when Ashley made noise. She noted that since the girls were sisters that I should keep an eye on her hearing. I thought that sounded a little crazy, but okay.

I was disappointed though because the class we observed was not a good fit for Ashley at the time. The children were ahead of where Ashley was with speech and language. Then there was the expense which I didn't think we could afford.

Several days later the teacher from the school called to say they were going to create a class just for Ashley and another little boy. They had a scholarship fund that could help us with the cost. I was jumping up and down.

One morning I went into Heather's bedroom and she was sitting up in her bed not looking at me. I said her name, and she didn't turn around. My heart sank. I called the Ear, Nose, and Throat doctor, and rattled off the types of tests Heather needed as soon as possible.

It turns out Heather had the same type of hearing loss that Ashley did, but hers was severe to profound. I was told the hearing loss was due to genetics. It was not hereditary, but my husband and I both probably had a recessive gene that became dominant.

I no longer felt the guilt of thinking I caused the hearing loss. However, as a mom, I felt responsible. I now had the why I was looking for so I could deal with it better. I hated that this was happening to Heather too, but I knew there was help available.

A month later, Heather was fitted for hearing aids and just like Ashley, she wouldn't leave them on. However, it was great that she got help with her hearing loss at ten months old versus age two like Ashley.

Early intervention is so important so that children don't get behind in speech and language. The earlier a child is diagnosed and gets proper help, the better off they are. I could not feel any stronger about this. Children also can develop behavior issues if they can't express themselves. I didn't want that for either one of my girls.

Ashley left her hearing aids in all the time now. After wearing them for six months she finally said her first word—up. I had been saying up, up, up when we went up the stairs at home, and she had been learning the word in speech therapy also. She said "up" while going up our stairs just out of the blue. That meant so much to me. I was so proud of her. What a special gift that was, and a joyous moment.

Ashley was already two years behind in listening and spoken language. I felt so bad watching home videos where I was talking to the girls, and they couldn't hear anything I was saying.

Initially, I taught Ashley five words in sign language to communicate a little better until she started talking. I used the signs for more, all done, cookie, sleep, and dirty. It helped.

Ashley's personality was shining through. When she got in trouble at home, she would turn her hearing aids off, and then not look at us. When she expressed herself to other kids, she made funny faces. It was interesting to see how she liked to be funny. She even liked to watch The Three Stooges. She tried poking me in the eye, so I had to show her that on the show they were really hitting their fingers above the eyes.

She quickly caught on at school and moved up to the class I first observed. That was a big deal. I regularly observed Ashley in her classroom. It was so helpful to know what she was doing during the day so Scott and I could reinforce the activity at night. Repetition was key. I also read to Ashley for about 45 minutes each night before bed.

By the end of the school year, Ashley was talking in three and four-word sentences. I found that unbelievable as she could say over 200 words. She had the desire to learn, and even won an award for the most improved in her class. *"Therefore, do not worry about tomorrow, for tomorrow will worry about itself. Each day has enough trouble of its own."* Matthew 6:3

During that time, the girls and I left the house at 7 a.m. every weekday to get Ashley to school by 8 a.m. in Atlanta rush hour traffic. It was usually bumper to bumper. Heather was attending the school too. Sometimes we made two trips to Atlanta in one day depending on each of the girls' schedules. I felt bad for Heather being in the car so much. She was making progress though. We were surprised when her first word was also – up! I listened to worship songs instead of rock and roll as I drove back and forth to and from Atlanta. It helped get me through that time. I was glad I was a stay-at-home mom so I could do this but wished I could have had both of my little girls' home to play with them and be the mother I wanted to be. But God had other plans.

My dad said he was proud of me for doing all of this. I told him I did not have a choice. I really didn't understand where he was coming from because I didn't think I had a choice in getting my daughter's help. I saw it as that was what I had been given, and it was my responsibility to do everything I could.

I was not as emotional about the hearing loss as when I first found out about it. I had surrendered and given it to God. I felt honored by God's trust that He chose me and Scott to be the girls' parents.

When I got overwhelmed, I reminded myself to just take it day by day. I felt so much stronger just being in God's word by continuing to do Bible studies and praying. My faith kept me going.

The Blessing School Brings

"For I know the plans I have for you," declares the Lord, "plans to prosper you and not harm you, plans to give you hope and a future." Jeremiah 29:11

Their school became like a family. We got to be around other children with hearing loss, their families, the staff, and the wonderful teachers. We all had a common interest. I felt accepted and supported like we belonged. It was a privilege to be there. The teachers were phenomenal and truly amazing. I was grateful to them all for their love, dedication, patience, time, and sharing their gift. My girls were talking because of them and the school.

Whenever my parents visited us from Ohio, they went to see the girls at school. I'm thankful the school was so gracious in letting them observe the classes and join in on birthday parties.

At that time, both girls had different feelings about their hearing aids. Ashley liked to cover them up with her hair, so no one saw them. Heather wore her hair up in a ponytail and didn't care who did. I tried not to let them be ashamed of the hearing aids or who they were. I explained how everyone was different, and that was what was different about them.

Time was really going fast. Ashley was in school all day and Heather was in morning classes. I worked in the library as a teacher's aide for a tuition credit. I met other Moms who were doing the same thing.

I liked seeing my kids in the school hallways from time to time. As I was walking through the cafeteria one day, I glanced ahead of me. I saw this little girl wearing a long adult t-shirt way down past her knees skipping from one end of the hallway to the other. I thought she was probably coming from the art room and looked like she was enjoying life. I looked again with surprise, and said to myself, "She's mine!" as I got a big smile on my face. It was Ashley. She looked so precious.

Besides being a teacher's aide, I volunteered for many events to help raise money for the school. I especially loved the field trips so I could spend more time with my girls.

Choosing Surgery

By the time Heather was four, she was out on the swing singing to God at the top of her lungs. That made me so happy as I wanted my girls to know God and Jesus. Heather was always doing something cute and funny. She was very sweet too.

At school, Heather was tested to see how far she had come with speech, language, and auditory skills from the previous school year. As she didn't progress enough, they suggested a cochlear implant.

I didn't really want her to have major surgery because she is my child. It was not like she had a broken leg that needed to be fixed. It was not clear cut. It was surgery inside her head.

Crying on the way home, I asked God what I should do. I heard Him say, "Do what's best for Heather, not you." Wow. I didn't want to be fearful or selfish. I trusted Him completely with it.

I talked to my husband, and he supported me with the hard decision. I did not want my children to just be alright, I wanted them to be great. They deserved to have the best possible education, hearing technology, and all of the opportunity's life had to offer. You must be your child's advocate. I also had God's blessing.

Advocating for Your Child

Around the time Ashley was to graduate from her school, I noticed that she needed to read my lips when I talked. That was something new. She could no longer hear me if I were upstairs and she was downstairs. Also, she wanted me to turn my head around when I was driving, and I couldn't do that.

I thought she needed the cochlear implant also, but a few professionals did not agree, because her audiogram showed that she still had reasonable hearing in some places. I was really frustrated. I am her mother, and I knew something was not right. I was not going to give up. I felt very strongly about her needing surgery.

Unfortunately, you can't just give a mother's plea to a surgeon for this type of surgery. I had to prove that she needed it. One person came to my rescue—Ashley's speech-language pathologist who I also considered a friend. After working with her and two different audiologists over the summer, they discovered Ashley had a fluctuating hearing loss. Praise the Lord. I will always be grateful to the speech-language pathologist friend for her guidance so we could find an answer.

The new school year started. Heather was five years old, and Ashley was six. It was so different that year. I was still going to Atlanta every weekday with Heather, but Ashley got on the school bus to attend the local elementary school. It was weird leaving town without her. I didn't like that feeling.

A Successful Surgery for Heather

Do not be anxious about anything, but in every situation, by prayer and petition, with thanksgiving, present your requests to God. Philippians 4:6

I had researched which surgeon was the best for Heather's cochlear implant surgery, and which cochlear implant company had the most success. Thankfully, our insurance company agreed to pay for the surgery and the cochlear implant.

 Heather had surgery soon after the school year started. It was very hard for me to just hand my child over to the doctor. My stepmom, Carleen, came down from Ohio to be with us. Heather did well. Better than me.

Heather woke up in the middle of the night and looked at her hair in the mirror. She had a long ponytail on one side, and a big bandage on the other. Heather put her hand on her hip, with a cute little look on her face that said to us, "What's with my hair?"

After Heather's incision healed, it was time to take the bandage off and get her head and hair washed. Seeing the dried blood underneath, scar, and her shaved head was hard for me to see. I'm sure it felt good for Heather since the bandage had been on for quite a while. Her Grandma Carleen brought her to a local stylist for a haircut. I'm glad she was there to take her because I didn't have the emotional strength as Heather is my baby after all. I was so happy to see Heather look so cute and precious with her new little haircut when she got back home. She loved her cute little styled bob on one side.

Since the swelling had gone down, Heather was ready for the audiologist to hook up the inside device with the outside pieces of the cochlear implant. It was so exciting to see Heather's first response to the new sound. She just kept saying the Shhh sound over and over and laughing at it. Evidently, she had never heard it before with her hearing aids. I loved seeing her so happy.

She was proud to go back to school with part of her hair shaved off and a new cochlear implant. The kids were familiar with it because most of them already had one.

One day Heather and I were standing near a water fountain. Heather got this surprised look on her face and pointed to her ear. She asked me what that sound was. It was the water running from the fountain. She had never heard it before. What an exciting experience.

The Same Surgery for Ashley

And the peace of God, which surpasses all understanding, will guard your hearts and your minds in Christ Jesus. Philippians 4:7

Four months after Heather's surgery it was time for Ashley's surgery. Even though I had been through this surgery with Heather, and knew what to expect, it still wasn't easy to hand Ashley over to the doctor. I was thankful I had my mom and stepdad, Dave, there with me from Ohio. Fresh out of surgery, Ashley appeared pretty beaten up. My mom stayed overnight with us at the hospital.

As mom and Dave left to go back to Ohio, my dad and Carleen were on their way to Georgia to see us. Even though we lived miles away from our family, I was thankful that they were so supportive. That meant the world to me. I loved them all so much.

Just like she did for Heather, Carleen took Ashley to the same hairstylist to do a cute little bob haircut for her too. Back at home, Ashley had that same proud smile that Heather did. Carleen got the girls to pose for a photo facing each other showing their haircuts off, and they looked so cute.

Bravely, Ashley chose to do a class presentation on her new cochlear implant device, and how it worked so her classmates could understand what she had. Those kids weren't familiar with one.

For Ashley, every sound around her was interesting as many of them she never heard before. For most of us, they were sounds we automatically know what they are, and where they are coming from. Things like rain, the dishwasher, or a dog barking in the distance. She wanted to locate the sound and learn what it was.

I am so thankful Ashley had the surgery. She hasn't had any more problems with her hearing since.

A Miracle

At the end of that school year, Heather had progressed so much that she could graduate. I couldn't believe what a difference having the surgery made. It was a miracle.

She went to our local elementary school for kindergarten that fall and rode the school bus with Ashley. After five years, I was grateful not having to make that drive to Atlanta anymore. It was all worth it though.

An Update and Musings

At the time of this writing, Ashley is 27 years old, married, and a proud graduate of cosmetology school. She has become an incredibly talented hair stylist. Heather is 25 years old, received her bachelor's degree, and is working on her master's degree. She is now a Registered Behavior Technician and is working with autistic children on their goals. She is engaged to be married soon.

Today, both Ashley and Heather communicate very well, and people don't know they have a hearing loss unless we tell them. Scott and I are both proud of all they have accomplished, and the wonderful women our daughters have become.

My experience has helped me to be more compassionate, empathetic, and understanding. I don't want anyone to feel as hopeless as I did. I don't believe in coincidences. We moved to Georgia from Ohio before the girls were born for my husband's job. God knew that our girls would have a hearing loss, and he placed us perfectly near one of the best schools in the United States. God had a plan for our lives. Not only did He provide for us, but He blessed us. I will never take that for granted and my girls know that too. I will always feel grateful. We persevered with God's help. I give Him all the glory. That is my mom's plea.

About the Author

Having her own personal health issues, Julie Jones believes that health and wellness is especially important, and wants to help people become healthier. She chose to become a consultant with one of the top CBD companies in the world, because she saw the benefits their hemp products made. They are the only company to have a CBD product with the hemp stamp of authority and recommended by physicians in the PDR.

She also has a business helping business owners with their follow up so they can build better relationships, get more referrals, and retain more customers.

Julie is a co-leader for a networking group called Xperience Connections, and a leader with Master Networks, a networking organization.

As a mother of two daughters with hearing loss, Julie knew her journey was going to be a different one. She wanted to share her story in this book in hopes of helping other parents deal with the emotional and mental struggle when learning their child has a physical challenge. Julie has 25 years of experience raising two daughters with hearing impairment and seeing them grow into happy, productive adults.

From the time she worked at the library at her children's school, and for Scholastic Book Fairs, she dreamed of her own book being on a shelf someday.

Contact Information

julieajones99@gmail.com
http://juliemontgomeryjones.com/

CHAPTER SIX

Running For My Life
By Gabe Cox

Just the Blues

"It's just the blues. Don't worry, it will go away."

This is what I heard in high school as I expressed the deep hurt tearing me up inside. Just the blues, I can beat that. This is normal, I thought. How I am feeling is completely normal.

With that thought process in mind, I plowed forward, moved myself cross-country to my Texas dorm room, and tried to push those emotions aside so I could enjoy my college experience. Maybe all these changes would be just what I needed.

I immersed myself into all activities because the busier I was, the harder it was for me to focus on my emotions. I was social and athletic. I made friends rather quickly and easily, but I always kept them at arm's length because I did not want them to see inside the true me.

Looking at me from the outside, you would have no idea of the turmoil raging within. I was cute, social, seemingly successful by the world's standards, and most of the time, the life of the party. I thought having so many friends and things to occupy my time could help pull me out of the darkness, but, ironically, it only made me feel more lonely inside.

A part of me felt so guilty for what I was experiencing inside because I was a Christian. I grew up knowing scripture and that God loves me and that His love is what truly matters. Growing up, I had a pretty good life. My family, though we had our issues, was good. My parents sacrificed so much for us so we could have and do all we wanted.

I felt as though I should have had enough faith to keep me from going down this dark path. Why would God let me experience this? What did I do to deserve it? I couldn't ask for help because people would judge my faith, wouldn't they? That guilt and condemnation had a grasp on my life that I could not release.

Exercise became my outlet. Fear of gaining the dreaded freshman 15 drove me to an unhealthy balance of exercise and eating habits. You could find me running five miles in the morning before classes, lifting weights in the afternoon, and playing pick-up basketball all evening. This unhealthy obsession quickly leaked over into my eating habits, and I would find myself afraid to eat, but, then again, when my emotions got the best of me, I'd binge on junk food.

Though I have always enjoyed working out and being athletic, it became a have-to more than a want-to. I had to run. I had to lift. I had to keep my weight down. I had to manage this demon inside. As my emotions became unmanageable, I substituted strict exercise and eating habits, as those were things, I felt I had complete control over in my life. Boy, was I wrong!

The Culmination

It came to a culmination my junior year of college. I had so many friends, and I had already accomplished some impressive accolades, but I felt more and more alone and out of control than ever before. I could not escape the negative thoughts of self-hatred. They slowly grew larger, overpowering me altogether.

The first time I picked up the knife, I didn't know what I was doing. I just felt so hopeless and unworthy, and I found myself beginning to slowly cut at my wrists, and as I did, I felt a new sense of control. For a moment, the slight pain I felt on the outside took my mind off the pain I felt so deep inside. Chipping away at the skin on my wrists or my thigh just above my knee became a ritual for me. It was my outlet, and no one knew.

I had one friend ask about the cuts on my leg, but I brushed it off and said I scraped myself, and she never mentioned it again. On the inside, I was crying out in pain, "Does anyone see me? Can they see the anguish I feel? Can they tell I'm trapped?" But I wouldn't let anyone in on my dirty secrets of self-loath.

The Breaking Point

Midway through my junior year, not too long before Winter Break, my mind began having thoughts of no longer wanting to live, and even though I promised myself I would never take my life, those thoughts were paralyzing, and they were real and hard to shake.

This was my defining moment. I knew what I was experiencing could no longer be summed up as "just the blues." This went far deeper, and I needed to face this disorder head-on before those sinking thoughts became my reality.

With shaky hands and an increased heart rate, I decided to pick up the phone and call our on-campus mental health services. The receptionist broke the news that they don't normally take new patients before elongated breaks, and, at that point, I broke down right there on the phone. My tears would not stop flowing. My heart sank with a sense of desperation, and, as if the receptionist could feel the same pain I was experiencing, she wisely said, "You need to come in right now." And that is exactly what I did that same day.

The psychiatrist diagnosed me with severe depression, anxiety, and ADHD. It may not have been too surprising to me, but I still felt some lingering denial. I felt as though my faith must not be strong enough because if it were, I should have been able to cope with the disease and recover without medication or outside help.

Road to Recovery and How I Found My Solitude

Admitting I had a problem was the first step to my healing, but the road was not easy, and I experienced many bumps along the way. The medication did help stabilize many of my symptoms and helped me function and sleep. The process itself was long and grueling, but I found myself on a life-changing personal development journey.

The most important lesson I learned is that my words are powerful, not in a manifestation sort of way, but that what I was telling myself, I eventually believed. The more I talked down to myself, shamed myself, beat myself up, the further I spiraled into depression. I had to reverse years of self-hatred. I can't pinpoint just one thing that led to my depression, but the more I dwelt on the negative, the further down I soared.

The simple act of changing how I talked to myself was the single most important therapy of all, and as simple as it seemed, it was one of the most difficult things I have done. I began searching for the promises from God about who I am in Christ and I began believing Him. Slowly my mindset changed, and I began to like who I was and saw myself through the lens of how God sees me. I traded the lies for God's truths.

I was on medication for about 18 months to help regulate my brain, but in the meantime, I worked hard to reprogram my thoughts, and when I came off medication, I never went back. That is not to say I never struggle with those defeating thoughts or feelings, but I now have tools in my belt to help me overcome them when they do try to creep in.

Looking back, I could ask, "Why me? Why did I have to go through this struggle?" However, instead of focusing on the "what ifs," I choose to believe God wanted to use this painful journey for good. All along the way, he was refining me so He could use me for His glory. I now use my message to inspire others to step into that fire of refinement, be okay asking for help, and encourage them to make it through the other side stronger.

Once I got a hold of my emotions and found balance again, running remained a part of my life. I began to find fulfillment in my time outside. It became my peaceful time, my solitude time, and my reflection time. Running went from a chore and something I could use as a form of control to a joy and an activity that I found a passion in.

It drew me closer to God, as He would use that time to whisper His truths to me. His beauty and creation surrounded me as my relationship with Him grew on each run.

A New Dream

After competing in my first marathon, a new dream birthed inside me - a dream to qualify for - and run - the Boston Marathon. I took all the mental training and success principles I had been learning and was ready to use them to achieve my dream.

Historically, the Boston Marathon is an iconic race many runners only dream about. Besides not being easy to qualify for, many are not willing to do the necessary work to get there. The qualifications are based on your previous marathon time, age, and gender. However, hitting a qualifying time does not guarantee you an entrance into the race. You need to also be among the fastest in your age group since there is a limited field size.

This dream became a burn for me because I realized that if I could do it, I could do anything I set my mind to. My boys were young, and as they were beginning to get out of the diaper stage, I began to have a longing to do something for me. Initially, when I moved into motherhood, I had placed my dreams on the shelf as a sacrifice for my kids, but what I came to realize is that they needed to see me win and bringing them alongside my goals is one of the best hands-on experiences they could have! I never want them to have to look past me to find their role model.

It took me about five years and three marathons, but I hit this goal of mine and stood on the starting line of the Boston Marathon for the first time in April 2016, as proud as could be. My first marathon time was 4 hours and 12 minutes, and to qualify for the Boston Marathon, based on my age and gender, I had to run a race in 3 hours and 35 minutes. This would mean shaving 37 minutes off my marathon time, which may not sound like a ton, but that is almost a minute and a half off per mile. When glancing at the facts, this seemed nearly impossible. I put in the work, and I learned what it took to have a dream, break it up into a simplified plan, do the work, and see it through.

Becoming a Coach

I knew I wanted to share my experiences and the lessons I learned with other moms, write a book, and begin coaching women as they pursued their own goals. Red Hot Mindset birthed out of this new dream. Shortly after, I published my first book, Mind Over Marathon: Overcoming Mental Barriers in the Race of Life, which is about taking a dream from the start to a flourishing finish and the journey of discovery in between.

Down But Not Out

Wanting to see what I was capable of, I trained for another personal best marathon time. In the fall of 2018, I not only hit my goal, but I smashed it, dropping another 12 minutes off my time and gaining another bid to the Boston Marathon. Life was gold! I was hitting goals and feeling strong.

That all came crashing down one chilly December morning when I went out for a pleasure run on what seemed to be a typical December day. Underneath a light snowfall were patches of ice that I could not see, and my foot caught hold of one of them, and I went flying. As soon as I hit the ground, I knew it was bad. I felt excruciating pain in my right ankle, and I curled up in a ball defeated.

An X-ray discovered a broken fibula, but the swelling was massive, so we could not do much immediately. On New Year's Eve, I received the devastating news. Not only did I break my fibula, but I tore my deltoid ligament and shifted my whole ankle out of place.

The surgeon dropped the surgery bomb on me as well as the news that my running would take a backseat for at least six months. No weight bearing for three months, a boot and a brace for another couple of months, and at the six-month post-surgery mark, I realized I would have to learn how to run again.

The injury tried to take me back to that place I was in college many years ago, fighting for my life mentally. I began experiencing those feelings of hopelessness and questioned why me? Why this? Why now?

Some of my first thoughts, though they were lies, were about gaining weight. My struggle with my relationship with food began emerging once again, and I fought eating, believing if I could not work out, then I couldn't justify feeding myself.

The good news? I didn't let this injury take me out. Because of what I learned and the refining process I went through in early adulthood, I had the necessary tools to combat these thoughts and mindsets before becoming strongholds in my life.

I am not sure if this injury was God-given, but it certainly was God-used. This slowdown gave me time to think and re-evaluate my priorities. I have always been here and there and everywhere, in multiple roles or jobs. When I broke my ankle, life as I knew it stopped, forcing me to slow down and make significant changes.

We aren't promised a life free and clear of troubles, but our setbacks can become our comebacks if we let them. This one helped me prioritize what is most important, where exactly I should be, and the calling God placed on my life. Though I do not know what the future holds, I do know God's ways are better than our ways, and in His will is the best place to be.

Building Mental Toughness

I learned three ways to improve my mental toughness and change my mindset from negative to positive. You can put these tools in your belt for when you need them too.

Tool 1. Change the way you talk to yourself: Learn who you are in Christ and stop believing the lies.

We can't change our self-talk alone, as we lack the self-confidence to do so. But there's good news! We just need to believe in God's ability to change and use us even though we don't feel capable, worthy, or ready. He is able and capable of doing all things He wills through us.

The lies are just that - LIES!!! They come from our enemy, the accuser, and we hear them all day long in our own thoughts and sometimes from other people. Do you ever catch yourself saying the following?

- I don't have what it takes.
- I don't have the time to invest.
- Someone else has already done that.
- It's never been done before.
- I could never do it.
- I'm not talented enough.
- I'm so far behind that I'll never catch up.
- I missed the wave.
- I lack the skills.
- I can't learn new things.

- I'm not a good finisher.
- I'm a failure.
- I'm just unlucky.
- I can't catch a break.

We cannot trust our feelings because they can change swiftly and fiercely. We can't let those thoughts come in and take over. Those lies will keep us planted right where we are if we let them. They will keep us from pursuing our passions and dreams. They will keep us from letting God work through us. They will keep us stuck!

I told myself plenty of lies while writing my first book, Mind Over Marathon! Here are just a few of them:

- There are already books out there about dreaming and goal setting.
- So and so already does it better than I can.
- I don't have the team they do backing me up.
- I don't have the finances to invest like they do.
- I don't have a publisher knocking on my door.
- I am not technologically savvy, nor do I have the latest and the greatest.
- I don't have the social network they have.
- I'm really a nobody.

Now, if I were to share my reservations and negative thoughts with you over a cup of coffee, you would slap me in the face and say, "Shut up!" Ha-ha, okay, maybe you wouldn't, but think about it. If I did say these things to you, as a friend, how would you respond?

You'd probably say something like, "You can't get down on yourself like that. You have a message that needs to be shared, and just because no one knows who you are now does not mean they won't in the future. Who cares if you don't have the team, technology, or finances others do? Work with what you have, and let God work through you. You can't let that hinder you from pursuing what you know you're called to do."

What do you think? Pretty accurate? So, I ask you if you wouldn't let your friends say those things about themselves, why are you allowing yourself to say those things about you? Why do you believe the lies?

Fulfilling our dreams starts with overcoming the ongoing lies we tell ourselves. Sometimes those lies develop into excuses or fears, but they are always stumbling blocks to our goals. We need to figure out a way to overcome them once and for all. Now, the truth is, the lies will always come, no matter how successful you become. They just show up on a different level. If you learn the keys to overcoming them now, you will be able to continue to do so later. The lies will no longer have a stronghold over you. Rather, you will have control over them.

Exercise 1. Change the Way You Talk to Yourself

This upcoming week note any lies or negative thoughts that creep up and write them all down. Keep an ongoing list, and at the end of the week, sit with that list and overcome each lie. Do this by writing the opposite truth next to each one. This will take some time, but I promise you it is worth it. It is eye-opening to see how much negative we pour into our minds daily or even hourly.

For example, to get your juices flowing we will take the lies I told myself while writing *Mind Over Marathon.*

LIE: There are already books out there about dreaming and goal setting.
TRUTH: *No one has told the story like I can.*

LIE: So and so already does it better than I can.
TRUTH: *So and so does it the way that works for her. I do it in a way that effectively works for me.*

LIE: I don't have the team they do backing me up.
TRUTH: *I'm fully capable of independently marketing my book until I can build a team.*

LIE: I don't have the finances to invest like they do.
TRUTH: *I have just as much opportunity as they had when they got started, and I don't need much capital to get it off the ground.*

LIE: I don't have a publisher knocking on my door.
TRUTH: *Self-publishing gives me more opportunities to impact others in multiple facets more than just my book could, and I have complete ownership of my book.*

LIE: I am not technologically savvy, nor do I have the latest and the greatest.
TRUTH: *Google and YouTube are my friends, and they can help me fake it until I make it in the technology realm.*

LIE: I don't have the social network they have.
TRUTH: *It's a fun journey connecting and building an audience that I can inspire to dream big dreams and motivate to go after them.*

LIE: I'm a nobody.
TRUTH: *God likes to use nobodies.*

Now it's your turn. Take this next week to reflect on the truths that you establish in your life. If you need help, ask a trusted friend or family member to share some truths with you. Search for scripture to back up your truths. I love using verses because they are God's promises for our lives. His truths never change.

Be prepared to go back and re-evaluate when new lies form. Keep a running log of the truths so you can continuously combat the negative. The more you do it, the easier it gets.

Tool 2. Look outside yourself: Learn the art of gratitude.

According to Google online dictionary, gratitude means "the quality of being thankful; a readiness to show appreciation for and to return kindness." This sounds great, right? Can you believe that gratitude can turn your emotions from negative to positive? The more you use it, the more positive you will become! It is a powerful tool that you can use to change your perspective on life.

One of the best books I ever read, the first of many on my growth journey, came from going to the bookstore just after being diagnosed with my depression and rummaging the shelves until I found something that stuck out to me. The book was called Lord, Change My Attitude, by James MacDonald, and it helped me change my mindset of negative to positive through gratitude.

The story featured the Israelites and their journey to the Promised Land. They began grumbling about everything, the long journey, and the bland food and wished they were back in Egypt as slaves. Rather than focusing on all the provisions God had delivered for their travels, they chose to complain. Because of their ungratefulness, none of that generation set foot in the Promised Land.

When we learn to be grateful for what we have, we naturally begin to live in the positive. We do not have to pretend we aren't struggling, but realize in every struggle, we can find something to be grateful for, and that gratefulness will help carry us through to the other side.

Exercise 2: Begin a Gratitude Journal

Every morning I write down three things I am grateful for from the day before, and sometimes it's hard to think of something, but once I have my three written down, it starts me out on the right track. It helps me focus on what is good and lovely and pure and right, all things that God wants us to dwell on. Here are just a few lessons I have learned from keeping a gratitude journal:

1. Things could always be worse. I have it so good! Life is good, and I am blessed.

2. A positive attitude is a choice. It is a skill that can be acquired.

3. It's hard to be negative when writing down gratitude. Even if I was toxic when I started, I'm usually more positive by the end.

4. It helps me see others in a positive light. It makes walking in love much easier to do.

5. I'm quicker to forgive the wrongs against me when I write down something positive about the person who wronged me.

6. I've gained clarity about what is most important in my life and about things I can and should let go of.

7. I hold onto less stress and worry.

8. My gratitude journal can serve as a mood lifter. When I'm feeling down, I can go back to it and read through all the things I'm thankful for, and my mood magically lifts.

9. The key to true joy is gratefulness!

Now it's your turn! Take the next 30 days to start your gratitude journal! If you are not a morning person, that's okay. You don't have to journal your gratitude right away when you wake up. You could do it at lunchtime, in the evening, or even when you are going to bed. Choose the time that works best for you and try to make it a habit.

One option is to choose three categories you want to focus on and write one gratitude from each category daily. In the past, I have selected to write something positive about my husband, kids, and life. Now, however, I just write three things down without a specific category. You get to choose which way is best for you.

After 30 days, go back through your journal and see all the gratitude you added. Journal about your experience. What did you learn? Did anything change? Do you want to continue this practice for another 30 days?

Keeping a gratitude journal is a great reminder about the good in our lives. It helps us put into perspective the trivial things we are dealing with because, even though they seem insurmountable at the time, they are minor in the grand scheme of things. Gratitude helps us see that we have a great life already!

Tool 3. Don't go at it alone: Choose to surround yourself with a positive association and mentorship.

Have you ever spent so much time with a friend that you started talking and sounding alike? Maybe people started mistaking you for siblings? Did you know that's because you naturally become like those you surround yourself with most?

Do you have a positive association to grow in? Who are you surrounding yourself with? Do they uplift you, support you, and encourage you? Are they growing themselves and excited about life? Do you feel better about yourself after you leave them than when you arrived?

Ask yourself these questions about the people you currently surround yourself with. Are you intentionally seeking out positive, supportive friends who are not only excited about you and your dreams, but they also have their own passions so you can encourage them as well?

In the midst of my depression, the last thing I wanted to do was surround myself with positive people because I was miserable! I was ashamed of how I felt, and I didn't want to let anyone in. However, this was a lonely place to be. I did not begin to heal until I was willing to ask for help and allow others in.

Mentorship is huge! When I was willing to allow a mentor in and become vulnerable with her, she invoked truth and wisdom into my life, and things changed. I began to see my circumstances as opportunities for growth, and her past experiences allowed her to see my situation from an alternate angle that I could not yet see.

Association and mentorship are two key things, but they don't take the place of allowing God to speak in your life. Bring your emotions and pains to Him. He wants us to be vulnerable with Him because He can change us.

Exercise 3: Check Your Current Association

Take some time to answer the following questions to see if you, indeed, are in a good association:

1. Who are your closest five friends?
2. Do they uplift you, support you, and encourage you?
3. Are you willing to be open and vulnerable with them?

4. Are they growing themselves and generally excited about life?

5. Do you feel better about yourself after you leave them than when you arrived?

6. How have they added value to your life?

7. How have you added value to their lives?

After answering those questions, consider these:

1. Do I need to consider shifting my association in any way?

2. Is my association drawing me closer to my goals or further away?

3. Is my association generally positive or negative?

4. Which of my friends do I have a mutual addition of value with?

5. Where else could I look for the positive association I need?

6. Do I need to find a mentor to go deeper with?

Choose close friends who you associate with carefully. Make sure you provide value for each other and that you build each other up and help each other grow. Surround yourself with people who are further along than you are. Association is key. Choose not to do it alone.

Victory Run

So, you learn these three tools once and never struggle again, right? Wrong. Sorry to burst your bubble. Every day is a constant battle for your mind. These tools help you stay on the right track. Sometimes I have thought I need to have it all together; after all, I am a mindset coach helping women break free from their own limiting beliefs and use their God-given gifts to influence others positively. However, if we don't have chances to use these tools frequently, we will take them for granted and forget how to use them at all.

Think of your challenges as opportunities for growth and opportunities to use these tools to come out stronger. God never promised we would not struggle - in the struggle is where the refinement happens - but He did promise to help us through those trying times.

The depression I experienced in college and the ankle injury I overcame just a couple of years back, have been defining moments in my life. Though both were challenging and painful at the time, I have allowed God to use them to inspire others. My victory run will be at the 2021 Boston Marathon, where I get to prove that an injury doesn't need to take us out. It will change us, but is that a bad thing?

My newest book, Victory Run, launches in the fall of 2021, and I can share my injury experience and the grief process that goes along with it. I take you on a journey from setback to comeback and how God can use your troubles to become your message. Interwoven throughout are other mother runner's struggle/victory stories of qualifying for the 2020 Boston Marathon and why that race would have been deemed their victory run as well.

Final Stretch

God gives you desires in your heart for a reason. That dream you have contains a message. God likes to use ordinary people to do extraordinary things. We need Him to accomplish them because our dreams look scary and impossible, and they are! They are impossible without Him.

I have shared with you how I've used running throughout my life in multiple facets. As I dealt with my depression, running was something I could control. Then it became a learning tool and, ultimately, my message. I fully realize that your dream or message may not be running, and that is okay! Whatever struggle you are going through; God can use it and turn it into something beautiful. You can apply these same tools amid any adversity or even as you are going after your big dream!

To get to that big dream or overcome that adversity, we need to give up doing it on our own and let God in and let Him work through us. If we do that, when we hit the finish line, we can't take all the credit. Instead, God gets the glory. That is what it means to run for your life and dream big!

About the Author

Gabe Cox is a faith-based author, podcaster, and coach who uses her passion for running to explore ideas around mental training, simplicity, and goal setting. She is the founder of Red Hot Mindset and also an RRCA certified running coach.

She used the mental training skills and success principles outlined in her book, "Mind Over Marathon: Overcoming Mental Barriers in the Race of Life," to achieve bids to the 2016, and 2020, Boston Marathons. She continues to use these principles as she strives toward new goals in business, raising a family, and mentoring others.

She dealt with severe depression and anxiety in early adulthood, and through personal development and her deep faith, she was able to take back her life and come off all medications. In 2018 she dealt with a debilitating running injury that could have left her feeling lost and hopeless, but because of the principles she has learned and practiced, she was able to use her injury to become her message and inspire others not to quit when the going gets tough.

Gabe created a framework called the Red Hot Formula for Setting and Crushing Goals that she now uses to help other women pursue their own ambitions. Her mission is to help moms step into the fire of refinement so they can come out stronger and crush their goals.

Learn more at www.redhotmindset.com or follow her at @redhotmindset on Instagram.

CHAPTER SEVEN

Keep Moving Forward
By Joric McLean

"Gather ye rosebuds while ye may, Old time is still a-flying."
—Robert Herrick

On the outside, my parents lived a life resembling a Norman Rockwell painting in an unassuming bedroom community called Harbor Beach, tucked along the banks of Lake Huron in Michigan. Both high school teachers, my dad coached multiple sports while my mom taught dance and gymnastics. They were busy, high-functioning professionals with goals and dreams to achieve.

On Friday, March 26, 1971, the day I was born, that all changed. Years later, my dad said, "I went to the hospital with your mom, who I considered one of the most beautiful and creative people in the world. I departed the hospital with you, my first born, and your mom. She was never the same." That fall, we moved to a ranch-style house only a block from Lake Huron, in a tiny enclave known as Port Hope. It is ironic because my earliest memories had little to do with hope. We did not know it at the time, but my mom suffered from postpartum depression.

The Closet

Early on in my childhood, I watched my dad coach or my mom train girls at dance or gymnastics classes. On weekends my dad would travel with my grandfather to pick up new furniture for his furniture store. Most of the time, he was gone just for the day but every now and again, dad was gone all weekend.

That is when my mom would take my hand, lead me into my bedroom, and open the closet door. She would point and say, "Go in there and stay." I would step in, and she would close the door. There were some shoes and stuffed animals on the floor and a few clothes on hangers in the small closet. The only visible light winked at me below the door, shining in through the shag carpet. On many occasions, I saw light and dark twice under the door, meaning I was in there for two days. Banging on the door, yelling, and screaming did nothing. But I hugged and used my Raggedy Ann and Andy dolls as pillows.

I had no food, water, or a place to go to the bathroom. I could reach the very bottom of the doorknob, but I could not turn it. It would not have mattered, as my mom locked the door. I did my business in a corner of the closet less than three feet from where I was sleeping or sitting. After a while, it started to smell like my old dirty diapers in there. I hoped the door would open, just long enough to get something to eat, like a banana, Cheerios, or oatmeal. Most nights, I slept with my head against the door wondering what was happening on the other side. Without warning, I would hear my bedroom door open, footsteps, and just like that, the door opened.

My mom stood in the shadow of the sunlight that now drenched the closet. She took me to the bathroom, used a damp washcloth to clean my face, arms, and legs. Sometimes she put on new clothes, sometimes not. I followed her into the kitchen, where I was usually given a piece of fruit. I felt happy to be out of the closet. No more bad smells, and I could play with my other toys. Oddly enough, I did not raid the fridge or cookie jar seeking sustenance. I would pull a chair over to the sink, using my plastic cup to get a couple of glasses of water. Before I knew it, I could hear my dad coming through the door.

As far as I knew, every other kid spent a lot of time in a closet. I did not know any better. I created my own little universe in that closet with my Weebles, Fisher-Price Little People, and Raggedy Ann and Andy. I gave names to each of my toy figures, singing the Alphabet Song with them over and over again. I imagined us playing in the bedroom, the living room, or maybe even the backyard. I would move Ruff, my Weebles dog, and Snoopy, my Little People dog, in circles as if they were chasing each other. I could put two figures in the small car. Over time, every figure, even the dogs, got time in that car, driving in circles around me as I sat in front of the door. Although I had not started school, my imagination was blossoming. I spent hundreds of hours in that cramped area.

My mother's illness worsened. Her Christian Science upbringing forbade the use of drugs, prescription or otherwise. By now, she had full-blown manic depression with a dash of multiple schizophrenia for good measure. She continued to spiral. One day, after countless times of being greeted by my mother opening the closet door, to my surprise, it was my dad. He came home early, my mom was gone, and he heard my voice inside my closet. He bent down and asked, "Are you okay? How did you end up in the closet?" I said, "Mom." He made me some oatmeal and poured some juice. Then, he gave me a bath. He decided I was going to move in with my grandparents. I got food at 8 a.m., lunch at noon, and supper at 5 p.m. sharp. I never worried about my next meal. There was no fear of being in a closet, and as a bonus, I got to use the toilet whenever I wanted. I felt like the coolest kid in town. I made friends in the new town called Ubly.

My parent's marriage was dissolving like Alka-Seltzer. My dad was hoping my mom would take medication or see a psychologist. She would have none of it, and my dad received full custody of me. Back in 1976, unless your mother was deceased or a remaining member of the Charles Manson family, moms always received custody of their children. For almost six months, I did not see my mom. Then, I saw her every other weekend and six weeks in the summer, per the divorce decree.

New Rules with a New Stepmother

Soon, we moved to a mobile home with my dad's girlfriend, Kathleen, a block away from my grandparents. Within weeks, Kathleen ordered me never to leave my bedroom when my dad wasn't home. I thought, "Not this again." I thought maybe all moms or mother figures acted this way. I did not know any different. Things were not bad, though, because I was not confined to a closet. I had a poster of Fonzie from Happy Days taped to the back of my bedroom door. I woke up each morning to Fonzie giving me a thumbs up and his signature "AYYYYY." He made me think everything was going to be okay.

As I grew older, I grew wiser. As Yogi would say, "I was smarter than the average bear." I stashed a large Styrofoam cup and an olive-green Tupperware bowl in the closet in case I had to go to the bathroom. My problem solving and ability to think on my feet would make a huge difference later in my life. Another woman in my life, another room to be left in. No big deal. The big deal was the house my dad and Kathleen were building on the outskirts of the village. I had no idea what little explosions of pain and suffering awaited me in this new home.

While my first six years of existence were filled with moments of neglect, during the next four, neglect would be replaced by violence. The new home was spacious. My bedroom was large; there was room for a bunk bed, desk, dresser, spinet piano, and closet. We moved in when Kathleen was pregnant with my sister, Ellie. The basement was unfinished, and within the first thirty days of living there, Kathleen made this place a little house of horrors for yours truly.

A House of Horrors

Two weeks after moving in, I came home from school and noticed the garage concrete had been poured. The garage was built, needing only a concrete floor. Just a day before, I was playing with soldiers and action figures in that very spot. "What happened to the toys in the garage?" I asked Kathleen. She was doing laundry and replied,

"They are buried under the concrete. You should not have left them there." Two days later, all my toys were gone except for two large Tonka trucks. I searched everywhere before asking Kathleen, "Where are my toys?" She replied, "I threw them away. You don't need them." Confused, I retreated to my room to read. My action figures were entombed under concrete while the rest of the toys were heading to a landfill. I did not understand why.

Six weeks after moving in, Kathleen yanked me out of bed in the middle of the night while I was sleeping, dragging me into the hallway. She stopped long enough to open the basement door, then pushed me down the staircase, slamming the door as I careened towards the concrete floor. The wooden stairs felt comfortable to me as opposed to the cold concrete. Two to three days a week, without warning or apparent reason, she would do this. I never knew when it would happen. There was a ten second window between dead sleep and somersaulting down the staircase.

When I was young, my mom, being a gymnastics teacher, showed me how to tuck my chin when doing a somersault. Her advice came in handy, as it prevented more blows to the head from the stairs or floor. After months of walking around with bumps protruding from my head, bruised arms, ribs, and legs, the terror at night became as routine as brushing my teeth. At the time, my hair was thick and floppy, so I could comb it in a way that would cover up my head wounds. Long shirts and pants covered any bruises a teacher might see. I did not want to draw attention to myself. Sometimes I would fall off the side of the stairs, headfirst, slamming onto the floor, and

I was out like a light. At least I was getting some sleep, albeit I preferred it to be in my bed as opposed to a concussion.

When I was able to get back on my feet, I would walk up the stairs and try the door. Sometimes it was unlocked, and I would poke my head into the hallway before quietly sneaking back into my bedroom. More often, the door would be locked. I would sit on the fourth step. That step was far enough away, so when the door opened, I would not get hit again. If I was tossed into the basement around midnight, Kathleen might not open the door until 6 a.m. I would wait a minute to make sure she was not near the door. I did not want to get pushed backwards down the stairs. I would cautiously peek my head into the hallway to see if she went back to her bedroom or was in the kitchen. If the coast was clear, I'd high tail it into the shower and get my clothes on for school. It was also enough time to clean up before my dad arrived home from his graveyard shift at the plastics plant. My dad worked all the time, and I did not see much of him. During the week, he would drive a school bus in the morning, then operate the furniture and flooring store from 9 a.m. to 5 p.m. After 5 p.m., he would deliver furniture or install carpet until 9 p.m. He would arrive home, get a bite to eat, or maybe an hour or two of sleep, and do it all over again. Those hundreds of hours in the basement gave me time to think and read.

I snuck a book from our Encyclopedia Britannica collection into the basement, as I spent about ten to twelve hours a week there. If I did not get bounced on my head, I turned on the lights and read about ancient cultures and far-off places I wanted to see if I ever made it out alive. They included the Egyptian Pyramids, Stonehenge, the

Colosseum in Rome, and African safaris. It gave me something to do, gave me one hell of a vocabulary, as well as a base of general and global knowledge which would serve me well in later life.

During my bedtime prayers, I would ask God for protection against Kathleen. God, or whoever I was praying to, was not answering my prayers. Maybe I was praying to the God of useless miracles. Invariably, the next day would come, and more violence would ensue. Eventually, I stopped praying.

My school counselors were focused on me being raised by a single dad, which in their minds was doomed to be a failure. They felt I was destined for a life of crime, drugs, violence, or my favorite, all the above. They didn't believe a male could raise a child alone and having a stepparent could lead to more challenges. It was a small town; divorces were rare, stepparents and stepchildren even more so. A counselor would generally ask, "How are you doing?" and sometimes give me a test to take. I would talk about my schoolwork, but never about what was happening at home. I once overheard a counselor say, "We have to watch this McLean boy. He is not going to make it." I remember thinking, "What did I say or write that made this person say that? What did I put on the test that makes this so? Yeah, I am going to make it. You have no idea what I have been dealing with from day to day. I'm going to make it."

Spoons, a Meat Tenderizer, and a Knife

Right after school and before dinner, the routine was the same. I would enter through the garage door, walk through the laundry room into the kitchen, hang a right, and walk down the hallway to my room. Within minutes of reaching my room, Kathleen would enter with a wooden spoon, force me to the ground or hold me against my piano bench, whacking my backside. I would cry and ask, "Why?" She never responded. Still, it was nothing compared to the pain from a good tumble down the stairs. The persistent beatings took a toll on the spoons and my butt. Many of the wooden spoons would break, which would only enrage Kathleen more. She would push me to the ground, walk out, and re-enter a minute later with a large metal slotted spoon. My tail was full of welts, blood, and markings from the holes in the middle of the spoon. On a good day, I got ten whacks. On a bad day, she would wail away until there was blood spatter on the window from the blunt force. I cannot lie; it gets tricky trying to sit on a chair at home, school, or a bus seat when your butt is throbbing and raw with welts.

At some point, she would change it up and use a meat tenderizer. Every strike of that tenderizer hurt. It was not uncommon for me to go weeks with black bruises from my chest down to my tailbone. After 20 or more whacks on my back and ribs, I would be gasping for air. The pain was palpable, and in a weird way, I missed my old friend, the metal spoon. I was starting to warm up to the idea that getting my ass beat every day was going to be a way of life. The spoons and tenderizer were painful, but it was the knife, as Chef Emeril would say, that "kicked it up a notch."

All Hell Breaks Loose

It was a typical Tuesday. The bus dropped me off, and I trudged up to the garage and entered the laundry room. I immediately felt the force of something striking my head. My head ping ponged off whatever it was, onto the side of the washing machine and then the floor. I went nighty-night. I don't know how long I was out, but when I woke up, I was a bit dazed, hearing the drone of the dryer in my ears. I got to my feet, and I was holding onto the wall for support as I turned into the hallway from the kitchen. I felt a pull on my backpack, saw my shoes at my eye level, and in a second, I was once again on the floor, this time the kitchen floor. I was staring at the ceiling lights when Kathleen leaned over and said, "Get up, you little shit."

I rose as fast as I could. She was cutting vegetables with a large kitchen knife. She stuck the edge of the knife into my Adams' apple, enough to make me cough. "If you tell anyone, your mom, your grandparents, and especially your dad, about anything that happens in this house, this knife is going right through your neck." If her goal was to scare the living shit out of me, mission accomplished. Nothing says I love you like a knife to the neck. She made the same remarks and held the knife to my neck several times, but the first time was all it took to put me on high alert. Her final comment drove home her intentions, "I married your dad. I can do without you." I slowly nodded, peed a little bit, and walked down the hallway to my bedroom.

By age nine, I was nearing a breaking point with the pain and abuse. I was snuggled up in bed and was awakened to hands grabbing an arm and leg. Kathleen feverishly pulled me out of the bedroom into the hallway. Here we go again. The basement door was already open when she pushed me in the direction of the stairs. I was on all fours, trying to hold onto the hallway carpet, which prevented her from pushing me down the stairs. But a kick to the back of my head did the trick. Impersonating a human pinball, I cartwheeled down the stairs. Happy to land on the floor without any major pain, I was not prepared for the fun Kathleen had in store for me.

She walked down the stairs, something she had not done before. I held out my arms, trying to defend myself from another attack. She pushed me to the ground as my head said hello to the floor. So much for defending myself. She opened the sliding door and grabbed my shoulders and arms, throwing me outside. My head was spinning, and I was getting nauseous as I laid in the snow. Did I forget to mention it was winter, and it was snowing? This was not the best time of year to be outside, wearing only pajama bottoms and bare feet. I tried to open the sliding door. It was locked. Every door I tried was locked. I was freezing. My feet were numb, and every hair on my body was standing at attention.

Even as a child, my survival senses knew I needed shelter and heat, or I would be a goner. The only door left to try was a balcony door off the dining room, but I could not reach it. As my body was trembling from the cold, I managed to place a thick piece of firewood on its end. I stood on top of it and pulled myself over the balcony railings and fell onto the deck. I crawled on all fours to the sliding door and pulled the door open. I made as little noise as possible as I pulled off my soaked pajama bottoms and curled up next to the heat register on the floor. I am not sure how long I was in the fetal position, but eventually, I stopped shaking and warmed up. My dad's and Kathleen's bedroom was in the back of the house, far away from the dining room, but I never knew when or where she would strike. After about an hour, I tiptoed back to my bedroom, put on new pajamas and a pair of socks in case Kathleen wanted to send me out into the cold again.

I Make a Decision

As I laid in bed, I looked at the chair and piano bench where thousands of swats from spoons and a meat tenderizer happened. I got out of bed and stared out my window. The light snow looked beautiful. In the moon's light, I could make out my tiny tracks to the front door and garage door. I remember thinking how lucky it was that the dining room door was unlocked, or I would be dead.

At that moment, I decided it was time to open up and talk about the violent world I was living in. If no one listened to me, and Kathleen delivered on her promise to drive the knife into my neck, I was going to die sooner or later anyway. I knew I would be spending the weekend with my mom. Although her illness produced initial neglect, she seemed genuinely happy to spend the weekends with me. It was a safe space, with no yelling or violence. She picked me up at noon on Saturday, and by 1:30 p.m., I was at her place, playing with my Captain America, Luke Skywalker, and other action figures.

I knew I needed to tell my dad about Kathleen sooner rather than later. I did not know how he would react, so I held a meeting with my action figures at mom's place. With them, I formed a circle and took roll call. GI Joe, present. Captain America, Wonder Woman, Spiderman, Pulsar, and Evel Knievel. All here. Luke, Leia, Darth, and Chewbacca? Yes, but no Chewie. Where the heck was Chewie? I found him slumbering in between couch pillows. No time to be sleeping, my furry friend; we have a lot to talk about. I asked the crew, "Should I tell my dad?" I reached out to each figure and pushed their head or body forward as if to nod approval. Shortly after my meeting, it was time to go home. I said goodbye to my faithful band of brothers and sisters and hoped I would get to see them in two weeks.

In the car, my mom usually played music. I heard a verse from the Buffalo Springfield song, "For What It's Worth," and it stuck with me. I did not know who Buffalo Springfield was, and it took some years before I knew the song's title, but the chorus resonated with me. I took that as an affirmation that I needed to stop the madness and talk about Kathleen's version of child-rearing.

The Big Reveal

My mom's Torino came to a stop right in front of the garage. I saw my dad's white delivery van, so I knew he was home. I was nervous, but ready to spill the beans. My mom reached over for a hug and I squeezed her as hard as I could. She said, "I love you. See you in two weeks." I mumbled a shallow, "Um, I love you too." My dad was in the dining room and Kathleen was somewhere in the back of the house. My dad asked, "Hey there, my number one son, how was your weekend? Is your mom doing okay?" For a moment, I froze. I looked past my dad to the sliding door, the only open door during my night of Kathleen's freeze out.

With tears in my eyes, I said, "I don't want to live here anymore." He touched my shoulder and asked, "What do you mean? Did something happen this weekend? You okay?" As I bravely took my shirt off, I showed him the evidence of Kathleen's transgressions. My ribs and back were blackened with bruises, and as I pulled my pants down and turned my back to dad, he saw the marks on my backside. With a horrified look, he cried out, "Who did this?" My dad rarely raised his voice, but his loud utterance got the attention of Kathleen. I heard her bounding down the hallway. She clambered, "What's going on here?" I pointed at her and said, "She has been doing it since we moved in here, and I don't want to be here anymore." Kathleen said, "He's lying. I have never raised a hand to him. It is probably his mother. You know she's off her rocker." As she stepped closer, my dad declared, "Back off." That shred of validation gave me the gumption to say, "Look at the marks on my back and butt and then go look at that metal spoon. The marks are the same." In the middle of the spoon were three holes that looked like tic tacs.

My dad walked us into the kitchen and to the vase of kitchen utensils. He took out the spoon and saw how it matched up to the markings. He said, "Get your duffel bag and put your boots and jacket on." I had never heard so many expletives before or since come from my dad. Before I knew it, I was dropped off at my grandparents. A week later, I would be reunited with my dad.

As we moved above my grandfather's furniture store, I wondered about the consequences of my actions. I should have trusted him and said something sooner. I thought maybe I should have stuck it out until I was older and bigger, more able to defend myself. From the moment we left the house, I packed and stowed my memories away to be dealt with at an undetermined later date.

Looking Back

In college, I thought taking an elective psychology class might help me reconcile with the past and move in a more positive trajectory. My professor, Dr. Eugene Scholten, had an open-door policy, so I made an appointment to see him. He ushered me in and offered me some water. I took it. He asked, "What can I do for you, Mr. McLean?" "Doc, I've got more problems than a math book, and I would like to have less problems to solve after our meeting. There are about a dozen large Samsonites packed away in my brain. My goal is over the next four years to remove that baggage and graduate with only a backpack of issues to work on." Scholten smiled and replied, "I figured you weren't here to talk about the syllabus. Why don't you close the door and tell me your story?"

Within an hour, I unpacked suitcases of verbal vomit, filled with pain, neglect, and the repetitive question of, "Why me?" hanging in the air. It felt great to open up. After an hour, Dr. Scholten said, "I need to head to another class." I asked, "How much do I owe you,

Doc?" He said, "Nothing. You pay for the class, but the counseling is free." I was trending towards a degree in education and had no desire to get a degree in psychology, but I could not stop taking classes as it afforded me time with each professor for "free counseling." Most of the professors had been in private practice before teaching and would listen and offer insight. Some gave me books from their shelves to read. After reading the book, I would set an appointment to discuss it and how to apply it to my situation. Soon I became a psych major. Over time and a bunch of free counseling, I found a way to let go of the past. I also participated in some paid counseling with my dad. We had several hours of sessions where he talked about his regrets, about not seeing the signs, working through his, "I should have known" while I worked through my "I should have said something sooner." We were always close and in a good place. The time in sessions only made our bond stronger.

The Second Act: Lessons Learned

I was now looking forward to graduating from college, getting out in the world, and beginning a new life and path. Though scars remained, those terse memories were no longer herniating from large suitcases. They were manageable and fit inside a backpack, another goal of mine achieved. As I left college to pursue life in the real world, I achieved one of the rarest things in life—a second act. No time to rest on laurels or take on the "poor me" persona. As Andy Dufresne said in Shawshank Redemption, "Get busy living or get busy dying." I was not perfect, resolved, or made whole by the counseling. But I was good enough to get out there and compete for life in a way I couldn't up to that point.

As I was graduating from college, my sister, Ellie, came to take a tour of the campus. After the tour, her mom, Kathleen, came to pick her up. The exchange was brief but cordial, consisting of a hug and pleasantries. She said, "It's nice to see you after all of these years." I replied, "It's good to see you too." Prior to counseling, if someone predicted I would meet Kathleen over a decade after that last instance of violence, and it would be a pleasant exchange, I would ask them for some of the drugs they were taking. We locked eyes, and for a few seconds, I wanted to show my resolve that in her thousands of attempts to break me, she could not.

The nugget of wisdom imparted on me by Dr. Scholten was the idea that what my mom and Kathleen did to me had little to do with me. It was my mom's illness, which to some degree, she was unaware of, not a hatred for me. And it was either illness, insecurity, or her own upbringing that led Kathleen to inflict the pain. I found out that "the why" is an ever-elusive moving target, and you don't always have to know "the why" to move on. Did it make the physical pain and recurrent headaches go away? Of course not. But it helped me move on from the past, and that is all I wanted to do.

I learned something else from my psych professors about adversity being good for us. Living through the experience sucks, but that adversity could provide a framework of strength to lean on when the going gets rough. Although I have gone through hundreds of personal or work-related stresses and issues over the years, those tribulations have paled in comparison to what I went through as a kid. I learned most of the really bad times in my youth had positive implications too. For example, the hundreds of hours sitting on a staircase, sifting through volumes of the Encyclopedia Britannica, gave me an incredible vocabulary and a broad knowledge of thousands of topics.

My problem-solving abilities were also born from turbulent times. I had spent a lot of time alone playing with my action figures and thinking about life. The ability to think logically about a situation, with little or no emotion, was a main driver in career growth and promotions. Not much bothers me, so it takes a great deal of antagonistic behavior to get me in a position to strike back.

When I am frustrated, I quickly ask myself, "Is this worse than being left out in the cold to die?" My answer is always, "No." When I don't think about that boy in the cold, I can go into some frustrating rabbit holes of negativity. I am also getting comfortable with being uncomfortable. The unpredictable nature of life can throw us all for a loop. The unpredictability of when I would be placed in a closet, tossed downstairs, or pounded with a kitchen utensil, programmed me to expect the unexpected. Change does not bother me. Adapting and adjusting on the fly has led to successful relationships and excellent reviews from peers and bosses.

I have also learned from my dad to not overcommit to a bad decision. If something is not working, change course. You find your kid locked in a closet. Change his environment. When your son shows you his body of evidence illustrating years of abuse, get him to a safe place. Do not go down with the ship. Empathy was another trait instilled through violence. Putting myself in other people's shoes has made me successful in my chosen field of Human Resources. I quickly realized my childhood and schooling made working in this field a good fit. Being able to accept and embrace the unpredictable nature of change is a great asset that not everybody has. I listen, ask questions, and I attempt to understand what makes my fellow colleagues tick. On the surface, I only know about events that made our conversation a reality, but I often wonder what their back story is. Maybe things are going great. But maybe a fight with a family member, a parent being ill, or their kids driving them nuts caused the action that made their conversation with me, the HR guy, a reality.

Lastly, I am thankful for my knack for humor, for making light of things even during the darkest hours. As you might have picked up from reading my story, quick wit and well-placed one-liners have been in my arsenal for as long as I can remember. I have no problem making fun of myself or making a comment that would ease the tension in the room. My humor has proven a vital commodity, with improv skills during management meetings or dealing with employee relations make tense or difficult interactions a little more palatable and fun. This life did not start out fantastic for me, but through turbulent winds, I have managed to change tact when needed, and set a course for great adventure. Oddly enough, one of the many far-off places I read about after another night in the basement was Lisbon, Portugal. Forty-one years after first reading the name and location of this place, I am now a resident.

About the Author

Joric McLean grew up in Michigan, the typical Gen-Xer, a child of divorce, setting out into the world with his latch key in hand. Joric has had more jobs than most, and with them, more problems than a math book. Prone more to improvise than follow the rules he often helped create; he found himself in precarious workplace predicaments, but his quick wit, sharp tongue, and sometimes oft-putting one liners, saved his bacon on several occasions. His endless supply of movie quotes, song lyrics, and Joric-isms, have blazed a trail for a unique style of leadership in human resource work. He has been a member of an award-winning HR team and worked for a company voted as a Best Place to Work for several years. Joric and his wife Shelly, are living life to its fullest in Lisbon, Portugal, while their son, Alek, takes care of the grandpup back in Phoenix. Joric is also the author of the 2-volume set of Magnet of Madness, a non-fiction book of mind-boggling stories he's been involved with throughout college and his career.

Contact Information

https://www.facebook.com/groups/740504546522681

CHAPTER EIGHT

Redefining Our Beautiful Lives
By Lynn Brown

Each of us have moments in our lives when we question how we have spent our time and if we've done all of the wonderful things we were meant to do. A few years ago, I had one of those moments and called my sister, Ann. During our conversation, I told her that sometimes it feels as though I have done nothing with my life. She laughed and asked, "What are you talking about?" Ann then proceeded to rattle off a list of my personal and professional accomplishments, making sure to applaud every significant and insignificant moment she could remember. My sister gave me a wonderful gift with her powerful words. She reminded me that I had done many things in this beautiful life I had been given. She inadvertently led me to realize that all of us must take stock of our lives and peek into our past to see where we have been and what we've done.

By taking the time to review my life, I was able to delve into decades of decisions that deposited me right where I am today. I caught a glimpse of my own process that showed how I redefined my life when a change was forced, wanted, or needed. Through acknowledging my successes, reimagining this life, finding evidence of personal interests by examining my past, understanding I hold the answers to my future, making positive decisions, facing my fears, and using my own power tools, I was able to readily redefine my beautiful life.

In sharing my personal process, may this help to guide, encourage, and uplift each of us in our own beautiful lives, whenever it is time for a new adventure.

Acknowledge Our Successes

When we encounter that moment of self-questioning and emptiness, perhaps we should pull out our pen and paper and acknowledge our successes. Take the time to physically write down and remember all the good things we have done throughout our lives. The positive things. Once we start our list, it is quite surprising what we can remember about ourselves.

Identifying our own uplifting accomplishments and recognizing their impact helps reinforce our worth and self-confidence. Remembering the good allows us to move forward into our next chapter in life. And if some of those memories aren't so good? Ask ourselves how we emerged and did we take that unhappy time and grow from it. Even the most trying times can offer a glimmer of good. Always look for the positive results, no matter how big or small the experience.

When I was a senior in college there was a program for all the upcoming graduates, which included an appointment with a job counselor. The counselor asked me about my college experiences and if there was anything, I had achieved that I was proud of. There was one event that stuck with me that had been an unexpected success. I told him the story about a group of us that had formed a coed softball team to play in our college intramural sports program. Every one of my teammates was, what would be considered, athletic. Except me. Naturally, I was put out in the far-right field because there was rarely any action for that position. But I did not mind. I was happy to be there and participate in a new experience.

Growing up, both of my sisters were very athletic and spent most of their youths riding horses and playing sports. I, however, was concentrating on my social skills, sewing, and my wardrobe. Yet, here I was, at our final softball game of the season standing in right field. We needed one final out to win. The opposing team's batter stood at home plate as the ball came flying towards him. He hit the ball high and far. This was it. The ball was flying out in my direction. At that moment, I was thankful my roommate Mary had been practicing with me for weeks, teaching me how to catch ground and fly balls. I was ready. I looked up, prepared my mitt, and caught that fly ball. I was so excited. I had accomplished something new and contributed to the team win.

As insignificant as that may have been to anyone else, it was an accomplishment that thrilled me to no end. I wasn't sure I was capable of doing it. When I shared that event with the counselor, he was clearly confused. Expecting my response to have been of much greater depth and insight, he clearly thought I was inept. The appointment did not end well. I could see in his face he was ready for me to leave as he rattled off a job suggestion which I would never pursue.

Something important happened when I walked out of that meeting. I learned not to let other people define me. After graduating from college, I began a fun and fulfilling retail career. I worked my way up the ladder to become a buyer and spent that chapter of my life traveling from coast to coast and places in between. I became the director of my own life.

Begin to Reimagine Our Lives

Even though we all live under different circumstances and responsibilities, we can make the choice to acknowledge, appreciate, and be thankful for our lives and our list of accomplishments. I know there are certain times in life when we feel stuck in a situation, thinking our only path is to dig in and work harder to make everything better. Oftentimes, that is what we need to do. But, in the midst of all that hard work, we may forget to value ourselves and give ourselves the opportunity to decide what it is that we really want for our future. This is the perfect moment to ask ourselves, "What do I want to do with my life? What do I want the chapters in my life to look like?" The exciting news is that we are the only ones that can write those chapters. Amidst our busy lives, we must allow ourselves to take a moment to make decisions that chart our course in the direction of our goals.

During my senior year at Oregon State, I did my practicum in a state funded home for troubled boys. Since my degree would be in Sociology, that was to be my future direction. I had spent the last two years preparing myself for a career in social work. When a paid position opened at the boy's home, I applied. I was not hired. It was very disappointing but forced me to think about other career options. With $100 in my pocket, I moved from the comforts of my college apartment to Portland, Oregon for a department store management trainee position. As soon as I got settled, the boy's home called me with a job offer for the same position I had previously applied for. I declined. Little did I know at the time, but I had just made a huge decision regarding my career path. I reached a fork in the road and chose an opportunity to reimagine my life.

It is scary sometimes. We don't always know what we are capable of. But we are the directors of our own lives. We can redefine ourselves and pick our strategy to achieve our goals. It does not have to happen in one day, one month or even one year. Just reevaluating where we are and making the decision about our direction is a perfect beginning to get us started in redefining our beautiful life.

Find the Evidence... Examine Our Past

A few years ago, I was asked to participate in an online class for authors. I was in the process of finishing my novel Three... from beginning to end. The class was teaching us about ourselves and how to create our own environment surrounding our writing goals. Now mind you, I was not one of those people that was born knowing what I wanted to be in life. I had many fabulous chapters and careers before deciding to become a writer. Were there signs that I enjoyed writing? Yes. But I was busy with other endeavors. It wasn't until I had children that my writing truly took root. That was when I began writing poems, letters, notes, and short stories for the kids. I remember being asked at a sales conference to share one thing I had always wanted to do. My answer was to write a children's book. I surprised myself with my response. But guess what? That planted a seed that grew to redirect and further define my life.

Listening to ourselves and examining our past interests help identify the threads of our future that are quietly woven into our souls. Throughout each of our lives, we give ourselves clues about the things we love to do or want to be. We migrate, perhaps unaware, towards activities and jobs that interest us.

When I was a junior in high school, my interest in clothing drove me to apply for a job with a company that owned three retail stores catering to young women's apparel. They were all in the same mall, yet each store made its own statement. The first store, Raggedy Ann's, was brightly lit by overhead cans, offering fun and inexpensive clothing to the penny-wise teen. The second store, Next Door, was lit with pointed spotlights facing a wall of expensive unique attire, highlighted to attract the high end, sophisticated teen. The third store, Julie's, became the place for every high school girl to shop, with every trend and cutting-edge piece of clothing displayed to entice any girl that came through the door. The music was loud, and the lighting was moody and emotional, just like its customers. I worked in Raggedy Ann's throughout high school and returned for every holiday and summer break during college. By the time I graduated from Oregon State, I had worked in all three stores and loved every minute of it. The clothes. The music. The atmosphere. The discount. When college was over and it was time to pursue my next chapter, I chose a retail career. The most fulfilling job of my retail career was as a buyer for the Junior department. There I was, back with the teenagers. However, this time, I got to choose the merchandise for the store, not just sell it.

My childhood interests in sewing, social skills, and clothing, led me to a career I loved and enjoyed for over a decade. If we look closely, we can find evidence in our past interests that stirs our passions today. Looking back on the things we loved doing while growing up, can provide us with the keys to unlock our future. Redefining our own lives is within our grasp.

We Are the Answer

So, what do we want to do now? Or better yet, what can we do now? Perhaps our current responsibilities do not allow us to make drastic changes. Maybe we have family and financial obligations that must be met to put food on the table. Maybe we are in the middle of a life crisis and cannot pile one more thing on our plate.

Let me divulge one piece of advice that was given to me by someone with a great deal of life and work experience. Her advice was certainly revealing and has, on many occasions, prompted me to rethink my daily decisions about how I spend my time. The same woman who invited me to join her online writing class, gave us students pause with a comment that is worth passing on and remembering. Her conversation started out with the many reasons why some of her students could not keep up with the class assignments. She said, "You spend your time where you want to." Now at first, my thoughts, and perhaps yours, went to "No, I spend my time where I have to." Or "I spend my time where I need to." While both of those responses may hold some truth, her advice is a great reminder to pause for a moment and think about how we are spending our days.

Are we, at any time in our day, allowing ourselves to identify the things we love and give ourselves the ammunition to redefine our chapters? What are we truly dedicating our lives to? Are we headed in the direction to reach a place we want to be? The provocative part about asking ourselves these questions is that we begin to identify our goals and make decisions as to what we want our future to look like. We can be the author of our own chapters in our book. We are the answer.

Sounds easy, doesn't it? Yet, this can be a tough task. In the thick of life, we roll with the rhythm of its beat. That rhythm can take us places we never dreamed we would be. That includes good and a few not so good places. When we find ourselves in places we don't want to stay, the opportunity to see exactly where we are and identify what it is, we don't like is right in front of us. There will be situations for all of us that beg for change. We get to decide what that change looks like. Whether it involves making the changes immediately or with a well thought out plan, the decision is ours to make.

In my late twenties, I found myself working for an exceedingly difficult and controlling person who was not even someone I directly reported to. But being two positions above me and constantly present in the offices, it became challenging to enjoy work. This person chose favorites, entered everyone's office at will, and slapped a yardstick on desktops to announce his presence. The atmosphere in the entire division became divisive and there was an underlying fog of fear and anger. A few employees found humor in the insanity of it all. Eventually I had to make a decision. Should I stay or go? I did something I would not generally recommend to anyone. I quit without having another job lined up. Was it scary? Absolutely. Fortunately, a buying job with another local company opened up and within a month I had a different, better, and happier work environment.

Sometimes we do scary things when we are in unhealthy places. The older we get and the more responsibility we carry often prevents us from doing what I did. But these things should not hinder us from deciding how we want to live and making a plan to put ourselves in a better place.

The benefit of that lesson was that it allowed me to be in control. I may have been premature in my decision to quit, but it helped me realize that when I feel trapped, I need to look for the release button.

Decisions

Discovering that we can choose to make decisions about our own future can be immensely powerful. It is exhilarating in many ways. Yet each of us have lives that are entwined with current and lifelong loves and responsibilities. Be it our families, friends, pets, or a variety of other obligations, we must consider our current path with our future when redefining our lives. The decisions we make will impact those around us. It is critical to keep our decisions positive and well thought out.

Remember that when we are redefining our beautiful lives, we will have rough and smooth moments. We must try to make this a fun adventure. The adventure is meant to uplift the decision maker, inspire others to have the courage to find their dreams, and put us in the driver's seat of our lives. Just remember to drive carefully and watch out for those around us. Accidents do happen. When we finally arrive at our destination, there should be joy and celebration with and for us.

I say "should be" because sometimes that joy and celebration can be slightly delayed. In one of my own redefining moments, my husband was, seemingly, caught unaware by a decision I made, which had a huge impact on our life. To this day, I am not exactly sure how that happened, but I blame it on communication! Laughingly, I ask, "Whose communication?" Let me explain.

It happened when our kids were little. Max was seven and Anna was five. Greg and I were both working and traveling in and out of state for our jobs. My career path had led me out of retail and into sales. I was a sales representative working from home out of an office Greg built inside one of the stalls inside our garage. We had discussed on many occasions how difficult it was to keep up with the fast pace of our lives. Max was involved in baseball, soccer, and basketball throughout the year. Greg was coaching Max's baseball and basketball teams, with a couple of their weeknights full of practices and late dinners. Anna was playing Tee Ball and I was her coach. I was also "room mom" for Max's first grade class and Anna's preschool class.

We were busy and concerned about keeping up this hectic pace. We wanted to be involved with the kids both in and out of school. Moreover, Anna's skin tone did not look right to me. She looked anemic and pasty. I took her to the pediatrician repeatedly for blood workups to see if something was wrong. Everything always came back fine. But I knew with every cell in my body, that something was amiss.

But, at that young time in our lives, our days were so full, we didn't have time to figure out what decisions we needed to make in order to create a happier life for our family. Work, school, sports, and health concerns were engulfing our lives. Greg and I had engaged in numerous conversations surrounding my job. We had a full-time nanny we loved, but did we want to continue to grow with our kids at this crazy pace? We wondered if we could afford for me to give up my job and stay home full time to take care of our family.

After a few months of looking at our finances and discussing the possibilities, I was ready and nervously excited to make the change. Nonetheless, it was gut wrenching because I loved my career. The morning I made that irreversible decision, I laid down on the couch and agonized over the outcome for hours. When I finally pulled myself together, I got up and called the New York office. I offered to stay for a month or so until they figured out what to do with my territory. My decision to redefine my life was underway.

When I told Greg that night I had handed in my resignation, he was not the happiest of campers. Looking back, surprised, and scared are two words that come to mind when he reacted to the news. For the life of me, I could not figure out why he was so stunned by, what I thought, was a decision we had made together.

It took us two years to adjust to the loss of income. I took over the finances and made it work. Sometimes it was by paying a bill at the last minute, waiting until Greg's paycheck was deposited. Sometimes it was by dipping into savings. And sometimes, it was simply through prayer and hope. It took three months to embrace and accept the redefining of my new identity. During those three months, I did look back to make sure I had made the right decision. Yes, I had. Anna's health improved and our family embraced my new, redefined role in life. Only then did the joy and celebration follow.

Our own joy and celebration may be immediate, or perhaps come with a slight delay. But, whatever happens, we must make sure to do our best in communicating with those that will be affected by our choices. Keeping our sense of humor if something goes awry is always a better direction to plunge. We don't have to give up on our well thought out plan to redefine our life. By examining all our options and staying positive with ourselves and those around us, it makes the celebration all that much sweeter. Once we are ready, it's best to fasten our seatbelts and hang on!

Don't Be Afraid

Fear is an interesting emotion and most often linked with negative feelings or circumstances, rightfully so most of the time. Fear is a natural response to an unnatural situation. To me, fear is a tap on the shoulder that gives a heightened awareness of something that does not feel right. I respect that intuition and do not take it lightly. We all experience many different types of fear throughout the chapters of our lives. The type of fear we encounter when making personal changes can be debilitating enough to hold us back from moving forward. Stay positive. Review your plans.

If fear were alive in the physical sense, we could see our opponent and decide if we were going to let it get in the way of our new direction and decisions. Mostly, it is easier to deal with a physical reality. But fear hides in the crevasses of our body, in both lightness and darkness. Expose it. Determine if fear is creating a positive, thought provoking, and important key to change, or if it is just a naysayer. We get to decide. Dealing with fear can be difficult. But we can ease our way through our fears by taking small, calculated steps.

I pray a lot. I talk to God quite frequently. It is important for me to feel safe in the arms of God. Throughout my life, I have needed moments, if not hours of solitude. Most of the time, that solitude took place at home. But there was this one thing I'd desperately wanted to do yet was afraid to do it. To most of my women friends, my fear was completely understandable, if not a bit heightened.

Being a woman and living with this fear is something most men never have to think about because it is a personal safety issue.

I love the majesty of the Pacific Northwest. I live near many beautiful, wooded parks that are loaded with amazing trails for joggers, hikers, bikers, birds, deer, owls, coyotes, bobcats, other fabulous wildlife, and even the occasional cougar. My goal was to walk through the forest alone and enjoy that time to slough off the weight of life while absorbing the beauty of the forest. I wanted solitude in the forest. But I was afraid to go into the forest alone. So, I would always go with other people.

One day my neighbor and I took a long walk and ventured up a new trail. It was out in the open, bordered by a few houses and close to my favorite park. I was in the forest, but safely exposed to others if need be. I started taking small steps when I was walking by myself. I would walk halfway up the trail, then walk back down. This process continued for weeks. One day I stopped at the usual turnaround point and looked up towards the end of the trail. I could see sunlight and the peaks of houses clustered in the neighborhood at the top of the trail. I asked God to keep me safe and up I went. That simple little decision allowed me to shed a piece of my fear. Now I constantly walk up that trail for solitude. It has become one of my favorite walks, even though I still say a little prayer for safety and stay fully aware of my surroundings. I know this may sound like such a trivial life event, but to me it was monumental. Small steps. Calculated steps. Success.

Power Tools

Our most important and powerful tool is ourselves. We must dig deep to find the courage and strength to guide ourselves in the direction we want to go. It is all there. Each of us has been given the equipment to redirect our lives and create the beautiful lives we imagined. Consider the following gifts to be our power tools. They may present themselves in various strengths and weaknesses, but they can be found and nurtured.

- We have been given a life, including the gift of memory to be able to acknowledge our successes and appreciate the positive things we have done with our lives.
- We have been given the gift of hope that allows us to dream and reimagine our chapters of life to come.
- We have been given the gift of a mind that functions to help us listen when finding the evidence of our past that paves the way to our future.
- We have been given the gift of self-confidence to look for and discover that the answers to redefining our lives are within us. Rather your self-confidence be a seed or a well rooted, full grown tree, it is within.
- We have been given the gift of critical thinking that allows each of us to determine the best decisions for ourselves.
- We have been given the gift of discernment in order to examine our fears. Personal strength and resilience are locked in our bodies. Let's not be afraid to break down our fears and step towards our own personal goals.

Our individual toolboxes have a variety of additional, unique instruments to help each of us in our quest to redefine our lives. For many of us, we consider people to be power tools. Friends and family can affect us in a way that pushes us towards success. The slippery slope here is that these same people also can temporarily derail our fragile beginnings. We must grab support from our trusted and positive team, making sure to find humor in those that express cynicism.

One of my dearest friends called me an "author" the minute I started writing my first novel. I loved that. It was her enthusiasm and excitement for my new beginnings that allowed me to see how important positive support can be.

Then came the contrarian. When I mentioned I was writing a book, she laughed and said, "You can't write a book." I responded with laughter. My past had equipped me with memories and resources to lean on when encountering people like this. One of my mom's favorite comments was, "Don't let the turkeys get you down." We all need to keep that phrase handy.

And lastly, my writing class instructor told me that "I was a writer the minute I started writing my novel." What a confidence builder. Those are the people we all need.

It is essential to surround yourself with people who support and believe you can redefine your beautiful life. Savor their comments.

And Finally

We must give ourselves the gift of approval to redefine our beautiful lives and begin our new adventures. It might be a new revelation or something we have dreamt of doing our entire lives. We can only begin when we give ourselves permission to embrace the change. By taking the time to acknowledge, imagine, examine, answer, decide, and plan, we can grant ourselves the opportunity to write our own stories.

When I decided to write my novel, I designated Tuesdays and Thursdays as my planned writing days. I made sure to keep those two days open, free from appointments and commitments. Within a few months, my family, friends, and co-workers respected my Tuesdays and Thursdays as days I was unavailable. My friends would not even ask me to come out and play on those days of the week, referring to them as my "writing days." I stuck to my schedule, most of the time, and looked forward to using those specific days to create the book I desperately wanted to write.

By designating special times to pursue the joy of writing, I established a routine that became ingrained in the minds of all those who knew me. It also became customary for me to look at Tuesdays and Thursdays as my own days to create. I grew increasingly territorial about my "writing days." To this day, I continue to give myself those two days for new writing projects and other personal interests. It is truly amazing what we can achieve when we commit to a plan and stick to it.

Each of us has our own pace in life as we gather our unique plans and forge happily toward our dreams. We must grant ourselves the time to enjoy our decisions and the patience to achieve our goals. It took me three years to write my novel. I loved every minute of the process. From the first moment I sat down at my grandmother's desk to tell my family's story, until the last word was typed to complete the final paragraph, I was happy to be part of something I loved doing.

We must remain kind to ourselves and those around us as we pull together our ideas to redefine our lives. Through planning and follow through we can turn our thoughts into actions and our actions into the reality of our dreams. We are only one thought, one step, and one experience away from redefining our beautiful lives.

We have been given one lifetime of opportunities to find our joy and use our gifts to inspire others. I choose to be hopeful that my days will be defined by good decisions, uplifting experiences, and many happy moments. Even the days that still make me wonder, "What have I done with my life?" When I get to the Gates of Heaven and look into the eyes of God, I can only pray the picture of my life reflects a trail of love, humor, strength, happiness, and faith. And when I pass through those gates, may I look up again and say thank you.

About the Author

Lynn Brown lives in Kirkland, Washington with her husband Greg. After two wonderful careers in retail buying and sales, she decided to retire and enjoy every moment of her young family's life. This allowed Lynn to volunteer as room mom, team mom, and chaperone for as long as their children, Max and Anna, would let her. Lynn is also a church volunteer, gardener, and caretaker of their cottage, as well as a contributing author to The Lemonade Stand and the author of her novel Three: ...from beginning to end.

Contact Information

Threethebook.com
Instagram...lynn.brown99
Facebook...Three: from beginning to end

CHAPTER NINE

Getting Through It
By Dani Warren

Let me tell you about the worst day of my life. It was 4:30 in the morning on June 9, 2005 when the phone rang. Back then, we had land lines where the phone was stuck to the wall. On the other end of the line was my Aunt Melba, my grandmother's big sister, who was all of 4 feet 9 inches tall. Living with my grandparents in an "over fifty-five" community of private homes, Aunt Melba reported something terrible happened overnight. My grandparents had both been rushed to the Chandler Regional Medical Center. As my Aunt Melba recently had brain surgery and lost the ability to speak normally, her voice was a whisper. It took me several minutes to understand what she was trying to tell me.

At the time, my mother was undergoing treatment for breast cancer which left her foggy and extremely uncomfortable, so my Aunt did not want to concern her until we knew the full extent of the situation. It turns out that my grandfather, a vegetarian, had a heart attack (just days before his ninety-first birthday). Then, when my grandmother leaned over my grandfather to help him, she hit her head on the marble nightstand causing a serious head injury.

I burst into action and drove the forty minutes to the Chandler Regional Medical Center as quickly as I could, seemingly on autopilot. When I arrived, my grandparents were in separate rooms right next to each other. The doctors, nurses, and I agreed not to disclose the seriousness of the injury to either one for fear the worry could hurt any chance of healing or at least relaxation. My grandfather recited over and over how beautiful my grandmother had been on a cruise they took years before, and the red dress she wore. The doctors determined my grandmother had a subdural hematoma that could cause permanent damage, and we made the decision to airlift her to the Barrow Neurological Institute in Phoenix for diagnosis and treatment.

I expressed to the medical staff that under no circumstances could we let my grandmother know she would be flying. She had an unnatural fear of flying and this could put her in a panic. Unfortunately, she could not be sedated due to her brain injury. The doctors, nurses, and I kept our little secret from her, and we simply told her she was being strapped in for a special test. I went outside and called my mother for help. I was hesitant to make the call because she was not feeling well due to her intensive cancer treatments. Mom put herself together and came down to attend to my grandfather after picking up my great aunt while I chased the helicopter for fifteen miles to Phoenix in my car. By the time we got to Barrow, my grandmother's forehead was swollen to the size of a grapefruit.

On the worst day of my life, I was thirty-nine. I realize today this was the day when I grew up and became an adult. I did not even think about what I was doing; I just did it. I understood the gravity of being the backbone of the family for the first time, and I felt compassion for my mother and the responsibility she had been carrying for so many years.

I spent the next two weeks with my grandfather both in and out of the hospital and chauffeured him around so he could get his things in order. He knew he would die soon. My grandfather, Murray Warren, was the greatest man I have ever known. As the oldest grandchild, and with my mom working in the city, I spent many special years living with and learning from my grandparents. They taught me to read and write and I was reciting state capitals by the age of two. Sitting on my grandfather's lap on his big pink velour armchair is my earliest and happiest memory. My grandma was sassy. She would cook the most delicious food and sing and make me laugh. She used to tell me jokes all the time, "You know who's in the hospital? Sick people!"

My grandmother remained in the hospital for almost a month, and we now know the injury caused her dementia. She never remembered the painful incident and only had wonderful memories of her years with my grandfather after that day. A blessing.

My mother was just nineteen years old when I was born in 1966. The oldest daughter of one of only a handful of Jewish families in the town of Poughkeepsie, NY, she rebelled against her parents and ran off with an Irish Catholic guy at eighteen and got pregnant soon after they were married. They divorced when I was an infant, and I have never known my father. Mom left me with my grandparents in Poughkeepsie and made her way to Manhattan in search of a career, just like Mary Tyler Moore, who starred as Mary Richards, a news producer on The Mary Tyler Moore Show who became a feminist icon. Every other weekend, my mom would come back to Poughkeepsie to spend time with me.

I imagine how difficult it must have been in the late 60's for a young, single career woman with an infant to find any level of success in New York. While my mom was serious and ambitious, my grandparents were fun, affectionate, naïve, and worried about the dangers of the world all the time.

My mother was an incredibly beautiful five-foot seven-inch inch woman with great fashion sense and her blonde hair in a teased bouffant that was so stylish in those days. I remember her wearing the Gucci belt with the big G buckle with her wide-flare bell bottom jeans. I believe it was during these years she developed a hard edge; a survival instinct borne out of her need to succeed and be seen and heard in a man's world so she could prove her worth. I was living with Mom in a one-bedroom apartment on the upper East Side by the time I was 4, a latch-key kid who was let into the small apartment by the doorman when I got home from school. There was no such thing as day care back then, so sometimes a neighbor would watch me, sometimes there was a babysitter, but I do not remember their faces or names. I remember reading books, even the encyclopedia, until she came home from the office. Mom would tell me, "Life is hard. It is just about getting through it. Not around it, or over it, but THROUGH it."

Fast forward to 2009. The country is in the middle of a housing crisis with dire economic consequences for me and most of my friends and family. At the time, I was the Director of Marketing for a swimming pool construction company that works with home builders, almost exclusively. I watch the company president, my brother-in-law, reduce the staff from seventy-seven down to ten, and eventually down to zero, closing the doors and leaving me without a job. No more six figure income for me or the lifestyle that provides. As the primary earner in my household with a mortgage and expenses, the stress became overwhelming. My husband and I chose to walk away from the beautiful home we built since the home builder had gone bankrupt and they had halted construction in our subdivision. By this time, the property was worth less than fifty percent of what we owed on it. We made the choice to file bankruptcy in hopes that would relieve some of the burden and we looked forward to a fresh start.

As we moved out of the house and into a small apartment, I started a new job selling cars where I was treated like a cog in the daily grind of the sales mill. "What have you done for me lately?" was the attitude the sales managers have. Because of all my life and work experience, I was left feeling lost and insignificant at the end of every day. I phoned my mother, looking for some guidance, nurturing, and love. Instead, she told me to "figure it out." I knew something was wrong with me. Why couldn't I "let it go" or "move on" like everybody else?

The personal and financial pressure was too much to bear. My husband was not helping to take the pressure off me either financially or emotionally. I realized I had failed yet again, and I left the small apartment and my husband and stayed at one of those crappy motels you can pay for by the month. I found a friend I worked with years before who was recently single, and we found comfort together living through these feelings of abject failure and melancholy.

This was the end of my second marriage, and I swore I would never put myself in that situation. You see, my mother had been married and divorced five times. I was not trying to go down that same path. Even though I wanted the divorce, I was miserable about it. I got another small apartment after liquidating my 401K with my new companion, Dave, who seemed to be a kindred spirit.

Five years earlier, my mother received a breast cancer diagnosis. After much treatment and many surgeries, she was pronounced cancer free in 2009. By 2010, I decided to help my friend and his catering company out for some much-needed cash. Before too long he decided to leave the business and allowed me to continue operations and keep the customers. This would turn out to be a blessing in disguise.

It seems as if I was just chugging along every day, and I had no purpose. I was not happy, but I was not particularly unhappy either. It had been this way for as long as I can remember. At this point, it is 2010 and I'm still with my boyfriend, so we put on our sweaters and jeans and got ready to head over to my mom's house for Thanksgiving dinner. I knew my grandmother would be there, with her dementia, along with some of my mom's friends. While Thanksgiving has always been my favorite holiday, family was starting to feel more like an obligation and less like a happy place for me.

My grandmother was feeding the dogs all the turkey, and although we kept reminding her not to, she continued to do it. She used mascara to draw her eyebrows on. It was simply horrifying to see my wonderful, fun-loving grandma turn into someone I did not know. My mother, usually always a great hostess who was well-made-up and looking good, does not look well. She leaves the party and all her guests and takes a nap in the middle of the festivities. When she woke up, we talked. She said she saw a doctor and he thought she was exaggerating her symptoms. To me, she looked haggard and her skin was very yellow.

A few days later, she called an ambulance and was admitted to the hospital. They could not figure out what was wrong, but her liver and kidneys were not functioning. Her body went into septic shock and she was moved to intensive care. As the medical staff treated her with an intense cocktail to kill the infection, my phone rang at 4 a.m. They informed me they would like to put my mother on a ventilator immediately. As a bookworm and my mother's only child and healthcare power of attorney, I wanted to read the documents she had left me to make sure I honor her wishes, but the doctors were pushing me to act quickly. I authorized the ventilator. My mother came out of the coma-like state and claimed she heard the doctors conspiring against her in the ICU.

Finally, my mom arrived home from the hospital. My new catering job allowed me to stay with my mom to help care for her dogs and distribute her meds. We went to several doctors where mom received some scans that revealed there was a large mass on her pancreas that was obstructing her liver, the reason for the sepsis. After beating breast cancer, my mother was diagnosed with pancreatic cancer. There is no successful treatment for pancreatic cancer. It is, effectively, a death sentence. I suggested mom and I go for a pre-chemo and surgery getaway. We flew to San Francisco and rented a car, drove through Monterey, and enjoyed an idyllic spot in Carmel. We drank Cosmos and laughed a lot.

Mom immediately headed into treatment, followed by the most inhumane surgery possible called a Whipple procedure which is almost 60 years old. At this point, I can't believe we can go into space, but we cannot find a more humane treatment for pancreatic cancer. My mom's spleen, gall bladder and parts of her liver and pancreas were removed, and her stomach was moved up and forward, so it looked as if she had a large mass under her breasts. The doctors told us before the surgery that it was likely mom would not be able to eat for many months after the surgery and to have a lot of Ensure shakes on hand. The day after surgery, mom was sitting up in her bed and beating me at Scrabble. By that evening, she was eating applesauce. All the doctors and residents were gathered in the hallway to watch, and they told me they had never seen someone recover so quickly after such an invasive procedure.

While we moved my grandmother into a full-time memory care facility just blocks away from mom's house, I took care of my mom's finances as well as working with my aunts and uncles to make sure my grandma's care was paid for. Sometimes the pressure was overwhelming, but I just kept going. I fought with Social Security and Medicare as well as the oncologist's office. Everything was a fight. I imagine what things would be like for people who have cancer if they did not have someone to advocate for them. Nothing was easy. It was an ordeal.

Mom, however, handled herself with dignity and grace. On her upper chest there was a chemo port, so she started wearing a fashionable scarf to match her outfit. We laughed that her closet looked like a Turkish Bazaar with all the scarves hanging on her belt rack. She insisted on going to a spiritual gathering every Saturday and continued to do a lot of the preparation for the gathering. Her brother and sisters flew in occasionally to spend time with her and to relieve me of some of the burden. Mom sought out alternative treatment and flew to Reno, Nevada three times for immunotherapy treatments. She received infusions of things to boost her immune response, but her white blood cell count was still high. I went with her once for four days.

In May 2012, my grandmother fell for the fourth time in her memory care facility, and we were informed she would pass soon. My aunts and uncles flew into Phoenix, and we had a family meeting to discuss pulling the plug on my grandmother. My mother was sick with breast cancer when my grandfather passed, and now she was sick when her mother would pass. It was not any easier to say goodbye to my grandmother despite the fact she had not been the grandma that I knew for many years. The whole thing sucked.

About eighteen months after her pancreatic cancer diagnosis, we knew my mother was already beating the odds. My mother knew she would die soon. She wanted to go to Israel with me before she passed. She started making plans. As Dave had been helping me with the catering business, it allowed me the time I needed to spend with my mom. By this time, I slept at her house, with one eye open in case I did not hear her breathing. I woke up at 4 a.m. every day to go back to my apartment to pick up Dave. We headed to work and finished lunch service. Dave and I would then shop for the next day's catering items and afterwards I would drop him off and go back to Mom's. Dave has been in the background but was supportive of me during the entirety of my mother's illness. He was seeing me at my worst and accepted me unconditionally.

I dug into my mom's finances, cleaned up after three dogs, fixed dinner, did laundry, and passed out my mom's medication, a cocktail of 45 different pills and potions. We watched TV. She liked Real Housewives of anything. She wanted to laugh at other people's misfortunes for a while. We watched American Idol, and she called in to vote for Daughtry. He got kicked off way too soon.

We traveled to Israel for twelve days. I carried her things, and we enjoyed the people, the places, and most of all, the food. She put extra hot sauce on her falafel, in direct opposition to what every doctor had suggested. Her energy level was low, but she had already beaten the odds by living for over eighteen months after her surgery.

The next nine months were a blur. Mom was very foggy and needed full time care. We had oxygen delivered to her house. We planned for arrangements with Hospice of the Valley, not for hospice yet, but for Palliative care. I let my mom's siblings know they should plan their visits sooner rather than later. They each flew into town, separately, for a week of time with my mom, and to give me a break. My Aunt Linda, who in the past had a contentious relationship with my difficult mother, became my mom's biggest support and mine as well. Meanwhile, Dave kept the catering business going so I could be available for my mom. Mom's hair never fully grew back the same way, so she decided to have me help her style it all spiky, like Anne Burrell from Food Network.

It was August 7, 2013. My mother was starting to reach the stage where it was difficult to digest her food. She was hungry, but her body was not cooperating. Over the phone, the doctors told me this meant the end is near. After another difficult night, I made the decision to call the hospice service for full-time nursing at the house. The first nurse was expected at 7 p.m. and would stay until 7 a.m., when a new nurse would arrive. I was afraid to shower, brush my teeth, or take the dogs for a walk for fear that my mother would need me when I would not be there.

My mother wanted to try to eat something at the kitchen table, a big deal since she had been in a recliner in her room for several days. I fixed her cottage cheese with some fruit, and we sat at the table while she ate. She asked me if I thought she had been a good mother, and for once she listened for my response. I told her the truth, which was that I was sure she did the best she could when I was younger. She was very practical and methodical, but sometimes I felt she was emotionally unavailable, and I always wanted more affection from her than she could supply. I spent a lot of my life being jealous of my friends who had moms who were home when they got home from school or baked cookies for the holidays. I now realized she was the perfect mom for me. She let me explore my own ideas of religion and spirituality. She taught me to be cynical and independent and fiercely loyal to my friends and family. She showed me it was okay to put on a brave face to show the world and come home and cry my eyes out. I told her all this and said she was a great mom.

She asked me if I was going to be alright. She told me she had done everything she wanted to do in her life. She reminded me the watch she was wearing was expensive so I should not forget about that. We went back to the bedroom, where I put her in her recliner, gave her a sponge bath, and changed her clothes. As she napped, she said she saw little fairies in a garden filled with pink and yellow flowers. She wanted to go there.

At 7 p.m., the hospice nurse arrived. Once she got settled, I allowed myself to shower and eat something. I had lost nearly forty pounds. Normally a size ten or twelve, I was wearing a size two. I settled into bed in the guest bedroom for the first time in weeks. Around 1:30 a.m., the nurse came into the room to get me. My mother had tried to get up to go to the bathroom and had difficulty doing that small task and was inconsolable. Mom asked if I would stay in the bed right next to her chair with her. I held her hand until she fell asleep. At 5:45 a.m., the dogs barking for their morning ritual woke me up. I took them outside and returned with Mom's morning medicine. As I walked into the bedroom, the nurse said, "I think she's passed." She looked angelic and peaceful. Her cheeks were rosy, and it almost looked as if she had snuck into her bathroom cabinet and put on some makeup although that would have been impossible.

Suddenly, after years of being in motion and always having a task to complete, I was paralyzed. I didn't know what to do. What came next is a blur. I called Dave and told him the news, allowing myself to cry. I got it together and called my Aunt Linda, delegating the task of informing the other siblings to her. I called my mom's best friend who rushed over immediately and helped me tend to the dogs. The little dog was laying on my mother's lap. The funeral home came to take my mother away. By 2:30 p.m. that day my Aunt Linda and Uncle Jim were sitting with me at the kitchen table. Linda, a notorious fix-it, started making lists. I was still wondering how they made it from Santa Barbara to Scottsdale in just a few hours. That was what I was thinking about, still numb to everything else.

I planned my mom's memorial. Actually, Mom planned Mom's memorial; it was up to me to execute her plan. She wanted a happy celebration, so I ordered lots of Pita Jungle and we played her requested playlist, including Hanson and Michael Jackson, at the spiritual center mom helped to decorate. Dave moved into Mom's house with me and we started making our life there. Eventually I left the catering company behind and got a job at a bank where I became the bank manager within a few months and life went on.

Now, as I look back at these experiences, I realize they represent my coming of age. I have learned a lot about myself and my abilities, capabilities, and weaknesses. I have become self-aware and extremely comfortable with who I am.

I have learned I am resilient. Resiliency means a thing is tough but flexible, that it can bounce back when stretched. I had no idea how tough I was until I was given the opportunity.

I have learned I am capable. Self-doubt never entered the picture when dealing with doctors or Medicare or even my sometimes-difficult mother. I simply forged ahead and learned as I went but doubt never entered the picture.

I have learned I am empathetic. Growing up an only child and learning to be independent from others for my own happiness often served to separate me from the realities of other people and what they experience. I am much more compassionate than I knew, and that compassion is a driving force in my life today.

I have learned I am an advocate. When the chips are down, no one is going to fight for you like you are for yourself. I know the difference between right and wrong. Just as I fought for my mother when she was getting the run-around from Social Security and her doctors and health insurance providers whilein the midst chemo-fog and heavily medicated, I fight for myself and Dave every day to continue to live our happiest and joyful lives.

I have learned I am free. This is a big one. I am free from living my life based on others' opinions of me, including my mother's. I honestly no longer care what the neighbors or my co-workers or family members think. I am free to be authentically me, and I never lose sleep over these things any longer. I am an adult, comfortable in my own skin.

I have learned I am funny. Mom and I laughed and laughed at her misfortunes and we allowed ourselves to be silly. It was cathartic. It still is. Dave and I are still together, almost eleven years later, in large part because we laugh all the time, every day, no matter what the world throws our way.

This is a story of forgiveness and reconciliation. Yes, my mother and I forgave each other for our past transgressions, but more importantly, I forgive myself for all the mistakes and poor choices I have made. I choose to live each day with humor, forgiveness, and forthrightness. I do not dwell on the past or what might have been. It is truly a blessing not to be burdened with the resentments and fear I had been carrying most of my life.

In the immortal words of my mother, Leslie Warren, "Life is hard. It is just about getting through it. Not around it, or over it, but THROUGH it."

About the Author

Dani Warren is an insurance agent representing American National Insurance Company, as well as a small business sales and communications coach and entrepreneur. She is originally from West Orange, New Jersey, and moved to Arizona in 1999, never looking back. She currently resides in Scottsdale with her partner, Dave, and their cat, Paulie.

Dani has been a sales, finance, and marketing manager, and her passion is using her experiences and expertise to help small business owners develop their dreams and improve their processes.

Dani has used this time during the pandemic to stop coloring her hair to let the grays come through, take courses, and increase her self-awareness. She has spent some time creating online content and courses for small business owners. She ultimately hopes to retire within the next five years to a cabin in Northern Arizona and start writing the book that has been in her head for all these years.

Contact Information

https://www.facebook.com/dani.j.warren
linkedin.com/in/daniwarren

CHAPTER TEN

Phoenix Rising
By Tina Krebs

I grew up in an average house on a quiet dead-end street in the northern suburbs of Pittsburgh, Pennsylvania, with a mother and father who loved my older brother and me so much. My parent's motto was work hard, play harder. As we knew how hard our parents worked, we did not ask for much. My dad was a machinist in a window factory, and my mom cleaned houses so she would be home when we got back from school or if we were sick.

My dad was a volunteer firefighter, and soon my brother followed in his footsteps. I was proud of them, but when I heard the sirens and their pagers go off in the middle of the night, I would not fall back to sleep until I heard them coming home and they were safe. Considering my father and brother were firefighters, it seemed only natural to earn my emergency medical technician (EMT) certification at age 16. By age 17, when my friends were busy partying, I was driving an ambulance and volunteering at Mars EMS. My mom, who I considered my best friend, soon received her EMT license. How many seventeen-year-olds can say they drove their mom to her first 911 call? I can.

Growing up, I was the most unathletic and accident-prone person on the planet. I broke every finger multiple times, forgetting to remove them from doors before closing them. I had multiple stitches for doing dumb things. When I was 11, my mom's best friend took me to meet her family in West Virginia. Her sister introduced me to Tae Kwon Do; I was instantly hooked. When I came home, my mom signed me up for Tae Kwon Do and it turns out that was the one athletic thing I was good at. While my friends were playing soccer or tennis, I was succeeding at martial arts. This chubby uncoordinated girl excelled at something athletic.

For 15 years, I worked hard to earn my third-degree black belt in Tae Kwon Do. Defying the odds would set me up for who I am today. Through my youth and martial arts, the values I learned include strength, courage, indomitable spirit, and perseverance. These are all values that helped me get through each day. I felt people underestimated me because I was a girl, overweight, or, let's face it, completely uncoordinated and clumsy. Despite this stereotype, I would stop at nothing to prove them wrong. Throughout school, I had excellent grades even though I felt it was too easy, and I was bored. I already figured out my future. I would graduate from high school, go into the army, and then become a police officer.

In my sophomore year, a teacher told me that planning to graduate early to go into the military was wasting my life and that I was a loser who would never amount to anything. I looked him in the face and said," Watch me." I went from 10th grade to 12th grade, completely skipping 11th grade. I was all set to go into the military; however, life got in the way. I met my first husband, the father of both of my children, AKA ex #1, and married when I was 19. Within our 15-year marriage, I completely lost myself. He told me I would never survive without him, that I needed him, and that I would lose my kids if I left. Just like everything else in my life, I fought back, especially because it was my children. Despite the threats, I left and rebuilt my life. I was happily working in a level one trauma emergency department. As I have been in healthcare most of my life, when a career-ending rare nerve pain disorder injury occurred four years ago, I refused to accept that at age 35, I was disabled and couldn't work anymore! I was devastated and so lost. That is when I discovered a different rewarding career. More on that later. Once again, no matter what life throws me, I never back down. I refuse to accept defeat!

In 2015, I married my best friend, AKA ex #2, who I worked with at the emergency department. My life would never be the same. Shortly after we got married, things became different. He was on his phone a lot more. And anytime I would walk into the room, he would hurry up and hide his phone. I knew in my gut; something was not right. One night when he was sleeping, I looked at his phone. It confirmed my worst nightmare. He was cheating on me. And to make matters worse, it was with a mutual friend, a former coworker of ours.

I confronted him the next day. He admitted it, and when I asked him if there were any others, he revealed a few more. I was devastated. I was sick. I was angry. I was furious. But, as this was my second marriage, and I had already put my kids through one divorce, I decided to stay.

On our first wedding anniversary, I discovered he was cheating on me with a former coworker the night before our wedding.

Somehow, I found a way to justify it. He had been good for a while, and then the drinking started to get worse and worse. As he became seemingly more and more depressed, he began drinking more and more. I had had enough. I gave him the choice of the bottle or me. I told him if he chose the bottle, that will be the most expensive bottle he ever chooses. He chose me. I naively believed him but also was extremely cautious.

Occasionally I would catch him sexting or sending photos to women. And again, I foolishly justified it. Well, at least he is coming home every night. I felt somehow that made it okay. I felt gross. I felt disgusted. I felt that this was all my fault. I felt that I was not good enough. Then, I was assaulted in a hotel hallway by two strange men. I had no idea who they were. Fortunately, I had a knife in my back pocket. And being a third-degree black belt, my instincts just took over as they were forcing me through the doorway of the hotel room. I broke free and pulled my knife and screamed. I pressed charges immediately. Both had a long list of convictions, including a plea deal for sexual assault of a six-year-old. They both were acquitted and blamed me, saying that I came onto them. Hearing the not guilty verdict was worse than the first assault. I was devastated. It took me a while to get over that. But then that grief that I had been harboring inside suddenly turned into anger. And then I was determined. I am a fighter. And I like to prove people wrong. I know what it means to be the underdog. This situation was no exception. I was determined to get justice my way. I did everything I could to take back and conquer every fear I had, including staying in hotels, being around people, and not trusting others.

On November 1, 2018, he was drunk again. By this point, he was drinking about a gallon of rum or whiskey in less than a week. Depending on the size of the bottle, he would go through it in a day. He was so out of control and withdrawn. I could not take it anymore. That night I received a spam text, some random number, and did not even read it. I just put my phone down to get a drink in the kitchen. As I left the room, my husband picked up my phone. It did not matter to me as I had nothing to hide. Something in the text triggered him. He was instantly infuriated as he thought I was having an affair; I was not. I explained it was a random spam text, but there was no getting through at all. He was drunk.

As I entered the living room, he grabbed me by the throat and slammed me down onto the couch, holding my hands above my head. Right there, he raped me on our couch and tried to strangle me. I was in complete shock. I have never seen that look of the pure ice-cold soulless person, hatred, and anger that I saw in his eyes. The more I tried to get away, the tighter he would squeeze me. When it was over, I could not believe what just happened. I did not report it until ten months later because I had no trust in the justice system. I told myself that it did not happen. Not again.

Life after the rape was different. I was stuck in a state of complete shock, yet utter denial of what had just happened. I could not accept it. I could not understand it. My mind just kept pushing it away. To add insult to injury, seven days later was the annual Marine

Birthday Ball. It was something we were planning to attend. I looked amazing and felt gorgeous in my beautiful gown. I felt like a princess, and he is off doing whatever and getting drunk. That is when I realized enough is enough. I thought about leaving him that night, but I didn't. The next morning, we came home. I was very quiet as I was so furious with him for how he had acted. After giving him the cold shoulder, I could not take it. I confronted him and told him that it was over. I did not want my children around him with his drinking problem. At this point, I asked him straight to his face why he did it. He knew exactly what I was talking about, but he stood there in silence. I said, "I asked you a question. Why did you break me? Why did you do this? Why were your hands around my throat? Why did you rape me?" He responded, "I don't know."

At this point, it was three days before Thanksgiving. I made him an offer that he could not refuse. And he agreed. I told him he needed to go to rehab or he would be dead by Christmas. He agreed that after Thanksgiving, he would go to the Veterans Hospital for detox and inpatient psychiatric therapy. My part of the bargain was that I would keep quiet about the problems we were having, and our break from each other would only be temporary. I agreed because it bought me some time. As the old saying goes, "Keep your friends close and your enemies closer." That is exactly what I did. I finally told two friends about our situation just in case something happened to me. I was constantly on edge as he had become suicidal and depressed.

Because of my martial arts experience and working as an EMS, I am able to think best in critical situations. After Thanksgiving, I told him he had a choice to sign in willingly for inpatient help in detox, or I would call 911 and have him involuntarily committed. He agreed to go because he knew that if he did not, I would reveal everything, and it was going to cost him everything. Being in detox was the safest spot for him and me. I anticipated he would be admitted to the hospital for a few weeks so I could get my exit plan in order. However, three days later, he signed himself out. I felt like the weight of the world was on my shoulders. But I decided I would play nice for as long as needed until everything was in place because I knew if he had any suspicions that something was going to happen, he might finish what he started the last time.

At home, he was writing me letters, multiple pages long, saying how sorry he was for everything he did to screw up our marriage. He promised he would be better and that he was done lying and cheating. This was surely not the man I married. Pulling information out of him was like pulling teeth.

I received a phone call three days after he was home from my mom stating she and my other family members were concerned about my husband and his drinking. They did not feel comfortable with the kids coming over when he was around. While she had no idea how bad things were, I completely understood and told her I would take care of it tomorrow. The next day, I fully intended to tell him he needs to leave by 8:40 the next morning. In the meantime, I received a phone call from my daughter's school that I needed to come in. Well, that is not good. When I got there, I saw my mom pulling into the parking lot. Saying I was completely blindsided is a complete underestimate. It turns out my daughter had acted out in school. She told the principal she just could not take it anymore and did not feel safe at home. One of those reasons was her stepfather's drinking, but the others were completely outlandish accusations coming from an angry kid.

Because she was stressed and wanted to spend time at her dad's place, I agreed as her dad literally lived across the street. Once she left the conference room, I told the principal and the other staff that I would remove my husband from our home immediately. When I came home and walked in the door, he was sitting on the couch playing on his phone and asked how the meeting went. I planned to remain calm, however, I did not anticipate the flood of anger I would feel the second I saw him. As soon as I saw him, I instantly started shaking because I had never felt that furious in my life! I looked him in the face and informed him that he had 10 minutes to grab one bag and get out of my house. He laughed sarcastically and asked if I was serious. I responded, "You now have five minutes and then I'm calling 911 and the police will be here to escort you out."

After he left, I changed all the locks on every door myself. I went into survival and protection mode. I had lost everything. I lost all my money, he stole all my savings, my car had been repossessed, and now I was losing my house. Because he did not keep up his end of the bargain, I reported the rape and abuse to the local police. I also reported it to the United States Navy as he was a 20-year career Navy Corpsman. I stopped feeling sorry for myself, and I started getting angry and taking back what again was stolen from me. I was devastated that the one man who was supposed to love, honor, and protect me was the one that hurt me the worst and almost cost me my life! And that does not work for me. So again, I decided to get justice in my own way. The best revenge is no revenge. Then, in August 2019, I discovered the unthinkable. My husband set up the first assault in the hotel hallway. There is no way to accurately describe the level of fury and rage I felt at that moment. But I somehow survived as I am a survivor. I was forced to move back home, which was less than a 10th of a mile from where I was living.

I have worked so hard the past year on healing and recovering and growing and learning my photography. I started my own photography business, Unique Photo Innovations, in Oct 2019. I specialize in all types of photography, especially capturing the raw, unposed emotions in life's most precious moments and letting the photo tell its story. It's more than just click and shoot photography, it's about creating a unique photography experience and making everyday photos into one-of-a-kind images that tell a story for generations to come. It is about the alchemy of reflection, transforming ordinary into a new illustration of beauty and depth. I have taken the experience of my own personal renewal and put that into my art.

I choose to keep fighting. I choose to never give up. I choose to be someone that takes a stand. I understand why people do not come forward after being assaulted, but whether you do or don't you still have the choice of how you live your life. There is life after trauma. You can heal. You can rebuild. However, you will never ever forget. I will never forget. It has changed me down to the core of who I am. But I made the choice to take back every single thing that they took from me. That includes my security and confidence. I take it all back. I took my power back.

I found my voice. I found myself. I found love for myself, love for others, and love for life. I am the best version of myself. I refuse to be a statistic. Let me repeat; I refuse to be a statistic. I was born to be the exception. I am the exception. I have taken back all my power. I have learned who I am. I have learned to love. I love who I am. I still fight my demons, and I am still not where I want to be quite yet! I have worked hard to get this far. It has been one hell of a transformation, and I love every minute of it.

Through this entire journey, I have learned so much and grown as a person, woman, and mom. I have a fresh outlook on life and see the world completely differently. The colors are brighter. It is as if I came out of a dark, abandoned, dilapidated factory. I have learned not to take things for granted as much anymore. I am more sensitive, but I am more sympathetic and empathetic to people and situations. I am the mother of two beautiful children who watched my every move and are my entire world. This was the hardest thing I had ever been through in my life. There were times I wanted to give up. I was exhausted and wanted to quit. Often, I didn't want to get out of bed. I asked God why he was punishing me.

You really don't know how strong you are until being strong is your only option. I was determined to make something good come out of this. They say everything happens for a reason, and God has a plan. For me, learning to trust the process is one of the biggest hurdles. I have renewed self-respect, self-worth, and I appreciate my inner beauty. Despite all the pain and heartache, I went through, I have found love. Throughout this process, I have discovered what true love is. I know it is worth it to look for a silver lining in every situation. By doing so, it starts a chain reaction. I have learned to turn all of my anger, rage, and pain into a fuel that will fuel the fire to prove others wrong. I refuse to be a statistic when I was born the exception!

Even though the local police department decided they will not press charges against my ex-husband, I am okay with that. I have found closure and made peace with my past. To escape, I found photography and photography found me. It has now turned into my gift. And my passion. I started my own business focusing on all types of photography and artwork, where I can create custom creations.

I know I am a fighter. I know that I am different. I do not want people's sympathy. I share my story because it has been one hell of a journey of ups and downs, twists, and curves. There have been days that I did not know if there would be a tomorrow. I know how strong I am. I know that the best is yet to come. And I have learned all of that through this journey. Just because I had no choice in what happened does not mean I do not have a choice in my future. They cannot take that from me. So, I built a better one.

When I submitted my first rough draft of this chapter to my editor, I did not have a title for it. A few days later, she sent my draft back with edits to approve. After reading my story, she suggested titling my chapter, *Phoenix Rising*. As soon as I saw her recommendation for the title, I was blown away. She doesn't know me personally, just what I've shared in this chapter. I knew it was perfect and meant to be! I was truly blown away because of what I am about to share with you. The story behind the Phoenix is that it rises from the ashes, a rebirth into something more beautiful, stronger than ever before. After I left my first husband, the first thing I did was get a tattoo. I had always wanted a tattoo; however, my ex-husband forbade me to have one. He said, "Only sluts and whores get tattoos." I wanted my first tattoo to be something special and have real meaning to me. I found the best tattoo artist in the area. One week later, I got my first tattoo. And you guessed it; it is a beautiful Phoenix spreading her beautiful wings as she rises out of the ashes transforming into the best version of herself. I have done this more than once. I have been knocked down and burned. Today, I have risen from the ashes of what used to be my dark, dismal past. I am now spreading my wings as I become the best version of myself yet. I am a Phoenix rising.

About the Author

Born and raised in Pittsburgh, Pa Tina Krebs is an award-winning photographer / artist and owner of Unique Photo Innovations, whose work has been featured in several publications. Tina is best known for capturing the raw emotions of life's most memorable moments as well as her ability to create unique photos that are not only visually stunning, but also telling the story from behind the lens.

Tina started her photography journey in 2018 as an escape and way to cope after ending an abusive and toxic marriage. With her strong will and determination, what was once her crutch has now become her passion and future.

When Tina is not behind the camera, she is a busy, single mom raising her 2 children, Faith and Joseph. In her spare time, she is advocating and raising awareness for survivors of domestic violence and rape while inspiring others how to live their best life after trauma.

Contact Information

Krebstm@gmail.com
www.uniquephotoinnovations.com
also on Facebook and Instagram

CHAPTER ELEVEN

The Alchemy of Forgiveness
By Nicole Harvick

"I wish he would have looked for all that I was instead of searching for all that I was not."—Nicole Harvick

Blindsided. According to the Merriam-Webster Dictionary, the definition is to surprise unpleasantly. The catalyst is common. A husband is caught cheating, a wife is blindsided, and a family is disrupted.

Over the years, I had several friends that were put through the stark reality that their spouse was cheating and the resulting upheaval of divorce. For some, I was their sounding board and voice of reason. I gave them a shoulder to cry on and offered words of wisdom. "Be strong," I told them. "You are smart, beautiful, and talented. It's best for both you and your children." I echoed the words, "You've got this," over and over as I advised them to leave their husbands because he cheated.

I was convinced by my own words. I can also remember thinking how grateful I was that this would never happen to me. And then something very unexpected happened. A husband was caught cheating, but this was quite different, painful, and scary! The difference was this time I was the wife. My husband was the cheater, and now it was my family that was going to be disrupted.

After twenty years of marriage, I discovered my husband had been cheating on me. I had texts, and I had pictures. It was indisputable. I was absolutely blindsided by this discovery and had so many questions, including "What do I do?" "What do I say?" "What did I do wrong?" It felt as if I had taken repeated punches to the stomach. I felt nauseous. But most of all, I felt scared! The counselor who had counseled her friends needed to be counseled. I do not remember anyone telling me that this knowledge of blindsided betrayal will take you to your knees!

As my identity was wrapped up being a wife and mother for the last twenty years, I now had some important questions to ask myself.

- *Who am I, and what am I looking for?*
- *Where do I start?*
- *What now?*

The Sickness Within

For most of my marriage, I had allowed myself to be silenced. My husband made it known that since he made all the money, he didn't need to do anything else. He gave me an allowance, and if I needed more, he called it a raise. This was so demeaning and humiliating for me. I had worked from the time I was 9 when I started babysitting until our second child's birth. But he who has the money often has the control. It was just easier to stay quiet so my girls would not see us argue. What no one saw was the slow death of my soul and my essence!

Having been sequestered away and never having used my voice much, I now wanted to scream. I wanted to lash out at my husband and the women he slept with. I identified most with the emotions of anger and rage. I was overwhelmed, and I did not know what to do. I felt as if my world was spiraling, and I was starting to become physically ill.

I began to experience debilitating migraines. I would scratch at my skin until it bled. My hair was thinning and falling out. I knew I needed help and I needed it quickly.

I started going to counselors, but all they wanted me to do was rehash and relive my experience which only allowed the pain to resurface again and again. I attended women-only support groups only to find more rehashing of the events, but now with added anger and animosity. I always left with more anger than I came with. I confided in a few close friends, but that always seemed to culminate with them telling me their story and then giving me their unsolicited advice. I often left more frustrated than when I came.

It soon became apparent this route was leading me to a dead end and I needed to take a totally different approach.

A Different Path

I have always been interested in the Meta-physical world. I would describe myself as an Empath and Intuitive. An Empath is a person that is extremely sensitive to other people's energy and emotions. We can understand other people's feelings as if we had them ourselves. I can often feel emotions through even a text or a phone conversation. An Intuitive can know or understand something without any reasoning process. It is a feeling that just comes over you, and you just instantly have knowledge of something. The following is an example. As I was working on a client during a Reiki session, I was guided to the right side of her body. I knew she needed extra healing in this particular spot. When we finished, I told her how that spot needed more healing energy. She then revealed that was where her cancer was discovered and where she had surgery.

I have always been sensitive to energies and am always on the receiving end of synchronicities. I started feeling myself being pulled to explore this path and to learn about healing modalities. My career had been in real estate. I had been a loan officer for twenty years and after that sold health insurance. It was a safe and practical job, but one I disliked immensely! It was then I decided to take a leap of faith.

That is when I started reading books. I devoured and digested everything I could find on self-help. I read and studied about meditation and mindfulness. I studied and became a Reiki Master. I chanted mantras. A mantra is a repeated chant that helps aid focus while in meditation or for general concentration. I loved the feeling I had as the chant resonated through my body. I always felt so calm, which was very empowering. I practiced mudras. A Mudra is a symbolic hand gesture.

I became certified in Energy Healing and Sound Therapy. As I started learning about and practicing these newfound modalities, I realized I had found my medium. It felt incredible to not only work on myself but to work on others. I enjoyed having them tell me how much I was helping them. I tell people I work on that they are healing themselves, and I am just a conduit for the energy.

Gradually I started to feel better about myself, and my health seemed to improve. I felt like I was starting to get a grip on my pain and the past. But I kept getting triggered by my memories and thoughts of the past. A lot of this came to me during meditation. Our bodies are brilliant. It remembers everything that happens to us. Often out of pain or fear, we bury memories we wish to forget. These were memories of feeling small. Of feeling as if I had no worth. Of always trying my best but being told I was lazy. Being told I was out of shape. I never felt as if there was any form of kindness or acceptance extended to me. These memories filled me with anger and rage, and I was not quite sure how to deal with these issues because I felt that something was still missing in my life.

As it turned out, that something was forgiveness...

My Discovery of Forgiveness

I have forever had a love affair with the Hawaiian Islands. I even moved there for a time after I graduated from high school. The minute you step off the plane, you feel different. Your senses are heightened, and your body energized. The island breezes are so soothing, and the colors are bright and vivid. You feel as if the island wraps its arms around you and embraces you. It always feels like home. I was excited to depart with my daughters for our trip to the big island of Hawaii, as this was to be my first time on this particular island.

Before I begin any journey, I always meditate and ask for guidance. I had no idea at the time how important this meditation was going to be.

I have spirit guides that I call in for meditation that offer me advice or give me direction. As I came out of meditation, I was told to "Feed the Stray." That sure seemed like an easy task to undertake.

After we had reached our destination, I started casually looking around for the "stray." I assumed the stray to be a dog, so I was observant whenever we saw dogs around the island. For some reason, nothing I came across or saw seemed to fit for me. As the trip progressed, I put the advice in the back of my mind.

Several days into our visit, we decided to hike the Kilauea Volcano. This is the most amazing hike which showcases the natural beauty of the island. It is lush, green, dense, and full of beautiful wildlife.

After hiking several miles, we came to a rope bridge. The bridge crossed over a deep ravine. As we were walking across, I heard my guides say to me, "Make an offering to the island." I immediately stopped and took some food out of my backpack. I then blessed the food and tossed it into the ravine. I was also instructed to give thanks to the island for allowing me to be part of such beauty and serenity.

As we continued our hike, I stopped for a moment, and I heard a loud rustling noise in the foliage. I looked to see where this noise was coming from. It was then that I noticed a small, hobbled bird.

My daughter Madi bent down to feed the bird, which ate right out of her hand.

I had found my stray!

What is Ho'oponopono?

As with everything, my time in Hawaii came to an end. Life resumed as normal, but I started to notice something that was a bit odd. I kept seeing and hearing this strange word. That word was Ho'oponopono. I not only saw it in print but also kept hearing it in conversations. I felt like I was being sent a message. I can now say I will be forever grateful that I paid attention and listened to what my message was.

Having never heard of Ho'oponopono, I thought I should educate myself on what this strange looking word was. What I discovered was that this is an ancient Hawaiian method of forgiveness. I had spent so much money and time on counselors, books, and classes that it seems doubtful that something so simple would work. I reasoned with myself that this method must not be any good because it was free. I was at a point that I felt I had nothing to lose.

Again, my guides spoke to me, "Just try it." So, I did. I would like to share it with you now.

Ho'oponopono is immensely powerful and consists of four phrases:

I Love You
I'm Sorry
Please Forgive Me
Thank You

Ho'oponopono is all about forgiveness, and forgiveness is all about obtaining inner peace and harmony. The English translation is "To make right." Forgiveness can release the invisible chains that keep us locked in anger and animosity. It can free us from the many burdens we no longer wish to carry. Forgiveness heals us. It is the most important gift that we will ever give ourselves. I decided to make Ho'oponopono part of my daily practice, taking anywhere from five minutes to an hour. It varies for each person. It is something that I utilize with honest and pure intentions. I started by lying in a quiet room and found a comfortable position, which was on my back. I selected the person I chose to forgive and used visualization to see that person. I closed my eyes and envisioned my ex-husband on a stage.

I then told him I forgave him for cheating on me. I forgave him for all the cruel and mean words that he had used against me over the years. I also asked that he forgive me for the same. I thanked him for the life he had provided me allowing me to be a stay-at-home mother. I told him I was sorry for the outcome of our relationship, which ended our marriage. I then sent him unconditional love. Not as a husband, but as a soul who not only needed love, but deserved love. After I had completed this process, I chose to sever the energy cord which connected us. This is an invisible cord that connects us to our higher self and people in our lives. In Hawaii, this is referred to as the Aca cord.

If you would like to try this, you will want to be in a meditative state to visualize the cord between you and the person you will be severing. When you find the cord, decide where the cut should be made and then visualize the cord being cleanly severed. It is important to remember that you might not be cutting off the relationship, but you are cutting off any negative energy that no longer serves you.

Why Should You Forgive?

There have been many studies that address why forgiveness is so important. If you research Dr. Haleaka Hew Len, you will find a story of how this man achieved amazing results with criminally insane prisoners. Forgiveness is for ourselves. It helps us grow as individuals and adds to our overall happiness. When we allow ourselves to hold negative emotions on the inside, it does far more harm to us than it does to the offender. Forgiveness allows us to live in the now. Nothing in our past can be changed. When you ask yourself this question, "What did I learn from this particular event?" you will often see things from a different perspective. It is then we can allow ourselves to walk our path of internal freedom.

I have described to you the Ho'oponopono process I practiced seven days a week. It was several weeks into my practice when I felt something incredible start to happen. My tears of sorrow began to cease. I seemed to have more energy. The inner doubt of who I was began to blossom into the knowing that I was important. Where there once existed anger, animosity, and hate, there now existed love. And this love was different. This love was a deep and unconditional love. And then something happened that I had never experienced, I realized this love was for me. I honestly never knew there was such a thing! What an amazing feeling this was. Forgiveness was the steppingstone to loving myself. My whole world shifted. I allowed my heart to expel the darkness and refill itself with the light of unconditional love.

During this practice, I also had a particularly important and poignant epiphany. I realized I was not sad for what I had and lost, but rather sad for what I thought I had and did not. This allowed me to understand my situation, and it gave me the clarity I needed to continue my journey of self-healing. It also taught me the most important person you must forgive is yourself. Blaming yourself for what you perceive as failures only lowers your self-esteem and blocks your natural flow of love. I encourage you to forgive yourself for what you did not know at the time you made the decision. And always remember, "It isn't failure. It's only feedback."

Forgiveness is For You

Before I discovered that what I lacked in my journey was forgiveness, I was a completely different person. I would erupt over the smallest infraction. I would cry over the simplest of situations. It was as if I had no control over myself or my emotions, and it was making me physically and mentally ill. I felt like I was living on the verge of a breakdown.

It is difficult to flow with the divine energy of love until you have released the negative energies of anger, hate, intolerance, and blame. When you realize you have no control over others, it is then that you begin to understand the importance of forgiveness. Whatever is happening to them internally is not a reflection of you but a reflection of what resides inside of them. Some people want to hold on to the anger inside them as if it is a badge of honor. Realize what lingers inside of you does no harm to the person you are angry with. The harm is being done to you. Forgiveness is not condoning the other person's behavior or actions. And it does not mean you have to forget what they have done. It is just releasing those heavy burdens that live in your heart that block the emotional freedom that you so deserve. Forgiveness takes place within your heart. It allows you to set your ego aside. It is your path to healing. It also comes from the eternal you; it comes from your soul. I have learned that loving yourself helps to illuminate the world around you. We are all connected, so shine brightly and allow those with the same vibration to find you.

You are Magical

"Watch the sparkle of the stars, for the soul is composed of the same energy that created the most important formation we wish upon."—Nicole Harvick

We are such magical creatures. We have the power to create that which we desire. The most important thing you will ever create is a powerful version of yourself. Learn to love your uniqueness! Embrace your fabulousness! Change is the only constant. Use it as a tool that allows you to morph from your cocoon and into the winged butterfly. Learn to forgive quickly and love deeply! Become aware that the only moment we have is now. As you are a gift, make sure you are unwrapped for the world to see. Live bravely and boldly. Use your voice and be true to yourself.

And always remember, "You are a horse of a different color. There is only one of you, and you're it. Live large and never forget to twinkle and to shine!"

About the Author

Nicole Harvick is the CFO of Don't Diss Abilities, an Arizona Non-Profit and 501c-3. Don't "Diss" Abilities was created to provide resources and activities to the handicapable community.

Together with her daughter Madi, they co-wrote the children's book " Boy on a Swing". This book is the true story of how Madi discovered her passion for helping individuals with disabilities.

Nicole is deeply passionate about Forgiveness. She feels that forgiveness is the key to releasing anger, animosity and resentment which can reside within you. She is equally passionate about the method of Ho'oponopono which she used to release these emotions. She credits this method with turning her life around.

She is the creator and designer of The Ho'oponopono Bracelet® which is made with lava beads and gemstones and is infused with Reiki, prayer and sound vibration.

She is a Reiki Master and is certified in Sound Therapy and Energy Healing. She is a lover of Moonlight, Magic and Mystery.

Nicole has 2 daughters, Madi 26 and Keely 18. She splits her time between AZ and SC.

You can learn more about her at

www.ofmanyworlds.com

www.omnisourceblog.com

https://www.facebook.com/nicole.harvick.90

https://www.instagram.com/nicolesharvick/

https://www.linkedin.com/in/nicole-harvick-4409a5a/

CHAPTER TWELVE

Hope Renewed – From Hopeless to Hopeful
By Kathleen Blair

I grew up at a time where little girls wanted to get married and have a family, especially if they were raised in an Italian family. Playing with dolls was my favorite thing. As I got older, I watched my girlfriend's dreams come true. I was always a bridesmaid, never a bride. Then I finally met the man of my dreams. Yep, I was the last one to marry when all my girlfriends were busy having babies and raising families. And I was the first one widowed.

We watch movies about how one event can change a person's life forever. We read about how an accident permanently leaves somebody unable to do what they did before. That is exactly what happened to me when my husband, Bob, was diagnosed with glioblastoma, a rare and aggressive brain cancer. Heck, at that time, I never heard of that type of brain tumor, let alone knew how to pronounce it or spell it, but it soon became our reality. When I first met Bob, I worked out, ate right, and rarely did the fast-food route. In contrast, Bachelor Bob was not very health conscious and lived on the convenience of fast food. During our early relationship and marriage, I cooked healthy meals. We played tennis a couple of times a week and bowled in two weekly leagues (no judgement here, I grew up in Michigan and that is what you did during the long winters). We even worked out together in our home gym.

In November 2001, Bob woke me up in the middle of the night saying, in gibberish, that he thought he was having a stroke. He was aware of the symptoms, as his father had just passed away from a stroke a couple of months prior. We rushed off to the nearest hospital. When I entered the hospital after dropping Bob off at the emergency entrance, he was still trying to communicate with the nurses in his gibberish, which they thought was a foreign language. As I realized what was happening, I yelled, "He thinks he's having a stroke!" Bob then was whisked away in a wheelchair to an examination room. After multiple tests, it was determined he had a clogged carotid artery.

His surgery was scheduled for the next day. Since it was the Saturday before Thanksgiving, we had purchased a couple of turkeys to donate to our church. They were in our freezer, and Bob knew I needed to take them to the church for needy families. He wanted me to bring them to the deacon's dinner being held at our friend's home, Pastor Saeed Hosseini, who would bring them to church that Sunday. When I arrived there, the pastor and our friends were about to eat. We gathered in a circle, joined hands as Pastor Saeed prayed grace over our dinner, and asked God to touch and heal Bob. While doing so, he looked at this watch and added the time, 7:34 p.m., to his prayer. We all agreed as we said, Amen.

While I was at the pastor's home, Bob's surgeon decided to perform Bob's surgery that night instead of waiting until the next day. Prior to operating, the surgeon ordered additional x-rays. Bob was upset about having surgery without me being notified. After the nurse took the x-rays, she quickly left the room. That is when Bob started to really panic. Much to his surprise, the x-ray revealed the carotid artery was completely clean! His surgery was abruptly canceled; Bob's speech became clearer, and he was scheduled to be released the following day. When I arrived the next morning, I learned about the evening's startling events which happened at, you guessed it, around 7:30 p.m.

Bob seemed to be doing great until three months later when he began having twitches that started in his right eye and would travel down his right arm, resulting in a couple minutes of speech impairment. At first, we thought it was stress related, but when the twitches came more frequently, we headed straight to the doctors to find out what was wrong. We went from one specialist to another for months. They performed numerous tests, it was the last MRI that revealed a tiny black speck, the size of a fine ballpoint pen dot. That's when we received the terrible news, from the neurologist at the hospital, that Bob had a brain tumor and was given only four to six months to live. Bob and I were literally speechless. The shock was so overwhelming we just sat there quietly as the surgeon left the room. Another doctor came in a few minutes later and asked if we had any questions. I can't remember which one of us asked if the tumor could be surgically removed. To add to the already devastating diagnosis, the tumor couldn't be removed as it was too small and not located in a place that they could access without causing more damage.

As Christians, our lives are built on our faith and trusting God. We were not about to accept the doctor's prognosis. Instead, we started praying that somehow, someway, God was going to heal Bob either by dissolving the tumor or by surgery. We were confident God would answer our prayers, as Bob had two prior miraculous healings, so what's another miracle!

When Bob and I first met, a recent skiing accident left him with a ruptured disk, three broken vertebrae, and a broken tailbone. He was told that he would never walk again – but he did, with constant pain. Being married to someone in chronic pain is no picnic. Bob refused to take pain pills as he did not want to get addicted to them. Together we owned a custom home business where we would spend hours sitting with our clients designing and pricing their home. When Bob would get up to say good-bye to our clients after a meeting, he would slowly rise and painfully try to stand. If I was out shopping or running errands and bumped into friends, it was always the same greeting, "How's Bob? How's his back?" I walked on eggshells on days he was in excruciating pain, and I kept praying somehow God would heal him. Twelve years later (you never stop praying for something you really want), God answered my prayers and Bob's back was healed. It happened at a Tuesday evening church service when Pastor David Friend asked everyone to come up to the altar to pray. As we were all in front of the altar, silently praying, Pastor Friend gently approached some of his parishioners and placed his hand on their shoulders or lightly on their heads and silently prayed. When we returned to our seats, Bob shared that when he went to sit down, it was the first time since the skiing accident that he didn't have pain. He was in such shock about the absence of pain that he didn't tell anyone, including me, as he didn't think it would last. Two weeks later, at our Sunday church service, he shared his miracle with Pastor Friend, who had Bob tell the entire congregation about the healing he received so they could rejoice in what God did. It was also to encourage others to keep believing in what they were praying for.

When we got the report about the brain tumor, it was not about whether God could heal Bob; it was when God would heal Bob. With a lot of prayer, eliminating sugar from his diet, and preparing alkaline meals, the tumor grew slowly until there was no more room for it. Eight months after the initial diagnosis, in late October 2003, Bob had a grand mal seizure in the middle of the night. He ended up in the hospital and surgery was immediately scheduled to remove the tumor. That morning of surgery, Pastor Saeed, my brother, and a few friends joined me to pray for Bob to have a successful surgery. After many hours, the nurse told us the surgery went well, and the tumor was removed. I was so happy and breathed a huge sigh of relief. My brother and I headed to the hospital cafeteria for dinner, as we hardly ate all day. As we were enjoying our meal, my cell phone rang. It was Bob's nurse, who explained post-surgery x-rays showed bleeding in Bob's brain, and he was back in surgery. We quickly headed back up to the waiting room and prayed.

Late that night, I was finally allowed to see Bob in the recovery room. He was still asleep, and everything seemed fine. After a couple of days, Bob had not gotten his speech back, nor was he able to move his right side. Apparently, he had a stroke sometime during or right after the surgery that left him paralyzed on his entire right side. He could not speak other than to say yes or no. Bob spent 33 days in intensive care, where he had a shunt put in his head for drainage and a screen placed in his groin to catch any possible blood clots. Each day I prayed Bob would survive each surgery, that his right side would start responding, and that he would begin speaking again.

Bob was transferred to a rehab center where he spent 90 days as they attempted to gain movement in Bob's right leg and arm. He also had speech therapy with the hope he could start forming words, but the area of his brain that helps with speech was injured by the stroke. During this time, I was with him ten to twelve hours a day, as he wasn't able to tell me what the doctors said when they saw him or let me know how they were taking care of him. He could not even communicate through writing as the stroke injured that part of the brain that formulates sentences. My goal was to make his time in the rehab facility as comfortable as possible. Family and friends visited, and we even had a potluck dinner there. Right before he was scheduled to leave the rehab facility, the social worker recommended I find a permanent care home to put Bob in as he would never get better. That was not going to happen on my watch. You see, I was raised that we take care of our loved ones. I was determined that Bob was coming home, and I would care for him. I will never forget how he cried when I told him the news. I cried, too, as I wasn't sure how I was going to manage, but I knew with God – *all things are possible!*

Fortunately, when Bob was at the rehab facility, my fabulous mother held down the fort at home, giving updates to family and friends and caring for our Springer Spaniel, Poncho. When Bob came home, mom and I cared for him. My mom loved Bob as her own son and frequently made his favorite meals. I'd often teasingly remind her that I was her daughter, and he was an in-law. Bob qualified for hospice having a terminal illness, and it was such a blessing to have a certified nursing assistant (CNA) visit three times a week to bathe him. We attempted to have as much of a normal life as possible. Every morning, I got Bob up and changed him. Then I would raise his hospital bed and help him eat breakfast. With my mom's help, I would transfer him from the hospital bed to the wheelchair and then from the wheelchair into his recliner. Thanks to our dear friends and my mom, we were able to purchase one of those recliners that will lift into a standing position. Wow, what a blessing that was! Transferring him was not easy, but we got better as the days went by. We would watch HGTV and enjoyed watching remodeling shows. I would tell Bob when he got better, we'd start flipping homes since he loved home construction and I loved designing.

As the holidays were approaching, I invited friends over for Christmas Eve dinner with us, as that was a tradition Bob and I had, and I didn't want that to change. He seemed to enjoy having friends over and understood everyone and laughed at their jokes. Months later, I invited my girlfriends over for a Valentine's Day lunch, and he really liked all the attention he received. During this time, everyone continuously prayed for Bob. Fortunately, he was never in pain. We had a routine going that was not the best, but it was the new norm for us. I was committed to overseeing his care, and I never complained or thought about what I was missing. I was my husband's advocate, and he needed me to be there for him. People would often ask me how I could manage to care for him, especially the bathing and changing him. I would politely ask them if they had children, and most often they did. Then I would remind them how they cared for them when they were infants, and later when they'd get sick and they had to clean up after them. When you love someone, you don't think about what you are doing; you just do what needs to be done because you love them, and you want them to be comfortable. It is an act of love, and I never complained. I was honored to be able to show my husband, and later my mom, how much they meant to me.

We periodically would go back to the doctor's office to check on his condition. In the spring of 2005, we learned Bob's condition changed, but not for the better. Apparently, brain tumors have roots, and another tumor was growing. As the tumor grew, seizures started again, with a bad one landing him back in the hospital. This time, the doctor was not recommending surgery, so he was released to go back home, and we prayed.

This new tumor was affecting the nerves that controlled Bob's eyes. It started the morning when the CNA came to bathe him. His eyes were scrambled when he looked at us. Bob could still answer questions with a yes or no, but we knew things were getting worse. That afternoon, Bob went to sleep and became comatose. I could tell his time was short by his breathing. I called my chaplain friend, Joseph, and asked my brother and mom to come into our bedroom to pray as the time was near. Although I was still standing on God's promise to heal the sick, I had to also realize there is a season to live and a season to die, and if Bob's journey on earth was over, I had to let him go. I whispered into Bob's ear that I loved him and did not want him to go, but if they came for him, it was okay for him to leave. God would take care of me.

I don't remember how long we stood around Bob's bed praying. Suddenly, Bob opened his eyes – now they were looking straight at me, but he did not acknowledge me. He turned his head to look up at the corner of the bedroom, and almost at the same time, he miraculously sat up in bed. I was in shock watching Bob do something he couldn't do for eighteen months and excitingly called his name, repeatedly, "Bob! Bob! Bob!" But his eyes never left the corner of the room as he took his last breath and fell back into his bed. I got to witness heaven coming for Bob. My husband was no longer paralyzed – God healed him and then took him to heaven. I witnessed an unbelievable miracle for our prayers were answered, Bob was healed, and his assignment on earth was over.

The following week is a blur with family flying in, friends bringing food, and planning for *Bob's Celebration of Life* service. I could not sleep and didn't have an appetite. I was numb, sad, and in shock that now my husband is gone. We spent every day together for seventeen years. I lost my spouse, my best friend, my soul mate, my lover, my business partner, my prayer partner, my tennis partner, my bowling teammate, my movie buddy, my dinner companion, my traveling buddy, and my theatre partner. Our wedding ring inscription is *"Two as One."* On May 14, 2005, my life, as I knew it, died with him.

I was accustomed to loss. I lost my dad in 1985, which was really the first loss that hit me. Sure, I lost my grandparents, but we sort of prepare ourselves for that because of their age. It is always sad, and you miss them, but the bigger part a person shares in your life, the larger the void when they are no longer there. I also lost two of my childhood girlfriends; one was my best friend who I shared everything with. I have great memories of making peanut butter cookies and watching the soap opera General Hospital during the summer, being cheerleaders together, and her maid-of-honor when she got married. It was painful realizing their lives were over when they were young, leaving a husband to raise their children.

In 2001, right before 9/11, my father-in-law passed away. In 2003, my mother-in-law passed away. After losing Bob in 2005, two years later I lost Poncho, who for fifteen years was my furry, four-legged son. And, in 2009, I lost my beloved mother. Every two years between 2001 thru 2009, I lost a loved one.

After my mom passed, I was now all alone. That loss was even harder as the house was totally empty. It was so hard being the one left behind, but I realized that we come into the world alone and we leave alone. My mom and I were extremely close and losing her was even more devastating than Bob's passing. Mom shared all my joys and sorrows, knew most of my secrets, and shared so many adventures with me. Her passing was the fifth one in eight years for me to grieve. Coincidentally, I started another grief class a month after she passed in 2009. I found that I needed the class as much, if not more, than those who attended. I wept and grieved right along with them.

In 2019, my chaplain friend and spiritual brother, Joseph, passed away. I met him the week before my husband died. In fact, he was with me praying on the other side of the bed when Bob passed. We became dear friends, and he mentored me as I navigated my way through Bob and my mom's passing. Each loss has been different for me, but the realization the same - they would no longer be in my life.

After a lengthy period of grieving and trying to figure out how to move on solo, I learned that my life was not over – just the seventeen years I shared with my husband and the long history I shared with my mom. I realized I could not take the broken pieces and glue them back together to be happy; I needed to uncover my gifts and talents and create a new life for myself filled with purpose. With lots of prayer, and a willingness to venture out, I began to take steps to create a new norm. I dove into reading all I could on grieving and started to journal again. Being alone, journaling became my outlet for putting my sadness on paper.

In late 2007, at my church, I was leading grief courses and doing private coaching for those who lost a loved one either from a divorce or death. Since nobody feels comfortable talking about grief and my friends knew I had been through plenty, they began referring people to me who lost a job, had gotten divorced, had a terminal illness, or lost a loved one. Since I had experienced so many losses, I felt extremely comfortable listening and guiding them as they began to uncover new directions in their lives. In 2012, I became certified as a Grief and Loss Coach and wrote a twelve-week grief course, *Journey Through Grief.* This course has helped hurting hearts learn how to process grief and create a new norm for themselves. It is extremely rewarding to see people smile again after months or more of them walking under a fog of grief.

I will never forget when a family came to my *Surviving the Holidays* class. They had lost their daughter to cancer and were now raising their two little granddaughters. The father, tearfully, pulled me aside after class and shared how unfair it was that his daughter died and not him. I could feel his intense pain of trying to comprehend the purpose. We can never understand why things happen the way that they do. I explained that his wife needed him now to hold the family together and that God entrusted his granddaughters to him and his wife so they could raise them to remember their mom and make her legacy a beautiful one they will carry the rest of their lives. As we talked, it appeared that the heaviness of his grief lightened. His posture gradually straightened, and his eyes widened. He began to see the importance of his new position.

Grief is a loss – a loss of a marriage, loss of a job, loss of a loved one, loss of one's health, loss of a pet, and many more. Grief takes on many emotions – abandonment, hurt, unworthiness, loneliness, emptiness, depression, hopelessness, and many others. These losses can be devastating. Unfortunately, no one teaches us how to deal with and process the emotions that accompany them. No one teaches us what to say to someone who is dealing with a loss. And well-meaning people can say things that hurt instead of help. Through my experiences and training, I can walk beside those needing help on their grief journey and show them there is a new chapter for them waiting to be written.

Everyone grieves differently. The deeper the relationship you had with someone, the deeper the loss and void. There are seven stages of grief: shock and denial, guilt, anger, depression, realization, dealing with the process, and accepting the new norm. The key is not to get stuck in the stages, but instead, process them so you can deal with each one and get through the journey. When people keep their feelings bottled up, it can create illness, depression, and suicidal thoughts. Some resort to medication and alcohol to numb their pain. Trying to escape the pain is not going to help, but only make it worse. Learning to deal and accept that your feelings are normal and temporary can give you the hope you need to continue to ride the grief waves as they come.

I never thought my spiritual brother, Joseph, would be enrolled in one of my grief courses. The death of his daughter to suicide was so unexpected and devastating for him. Now I was there to help him try to come to a place that would allow him to process his emotions as he walked through the grief journey. As a chaplain, he had performed many funerals and prayed for those that lost loved ones, but now he needed prayers for himself. Many years before losing his daughter, he lost a young son. He was no stranger to grief, but now losing another child became exceedingly difficult as it opened up old wounds. As he participated in class, I could see how it helped that he could share his feelings in a safe atmosphere where he could be transparent without being judged. He also contributed biblical scripture that helped many people in the group. It was such an honor to coach him through his grief journey.

Grief coaching allows me to utilize my career coaching experience. When I moved to Arizona in 1986, I became an employment job recruiter in the computer industry since I had worked in this industry in sales and as a National Account Manager with national contacts. I coached job applicants and Arizona State University students on job interviewing and did mock interviews with them via video. I provided constructive criticism, so they were prepared to do their best in an actual interview. I would also provide feedback on how they could rework their resume to get the attention of potential employers. In addition, I held interview skills workshops for a few local high schools teaching from a manual I wrote, Interviewing Skills 101.

In 2020 with the pandemic, I frequently received calls from those dealing with job loss. Many lost their businesses and were devastated, and as a result they were unsure what to do. The job loss course I developed covers how to deal with the emotions of losing a job, how to use those emotions constructively, how to narrow down positions that match one's skills, how to set new goals, tips on resume writing, and effective interviewing skills. I can see how God has taken all my gifts, skills, and experiences I developed throughout my life to help others through my coaching business.

These past sixteen years have brought me to a stage in my life where I feel I can now tackle anything life brings. Grieving over a loss also means learning to accept the change that has affected the life you have had. Change is difficult for most people. Most losses are not planned so there's no preparing ahead of time for it. It seems like your world is shaken upside down and you are left having to put the pieces back. But the pieces no longer fit where they once were. Whether it is no longer having the job you held for years, an illness that prevents you from doing things you enjoy, a divorce or a loved one that passed away, loss is hard, and accepting a new normal takes time. During the grief journey, you learn grief does not have a timetable or a measuring stick; one grieves to the depth of their loss.

Losing my husband left me with none of the puzzle pieces fitting back in place. Through my grieving process each day I got a little stronger and picked up a piece of my life and recognized that I needed to find a new place for it to fit. It did not happen quickly and some days I took steps backwards. But gradually I made it through as I clung to God's promises that He would never forsake me. He'd provide all my needs and the latter days would be better than the rest. My journey was hard, and it helped to have Joseph, who also experienced losses, to talk with as he understood and could encourage me to keep moving on this "new" path.

Although my parents, in-laws and husband are gone, I have fond memories of them. I carry them in my heart and am delighted when someone allows me to share their memories. I get excited when I introduce my new friends, who never met Bob, to someone and say, "They knew Bob before he was sick." No one can ever take my memories from me. Now, being able to help people deal with their loss is a way of keeping their legacy.

I treasure my memories and almost daily it seems that something reminds me of one of my loved ones. I can smile and not feel so sad. I can totally relate to Celine Dion's song, "Because You Love Me" as the lyrics remind me of what Bob would say, if he could have spoken to me during the months, I cared for him after his surgery. I was strong when my Bobby was weak, I was his voice when He could not speak, I had faith for both of us as I believed, all because I loved him.

I know I have been divinely led to become a Grief and Loss Coach. My tears have strengthened me, and my experiences have prepared me to help others find their way. As Bob's caregiver, I developed strength to take on things I didn't know I was capable of doing. And, after I found I could love again and met a wonderful man who loves and supports me in my choices. My journey through grief was hard, took time, but in the end, I found a new purpose and carved a new life filled with hope!

About the Author

Kathleen Blair has never been afraid of the word "no." Despite being the only woman on the Xerox Corporation sales team, she succeeded in sales as "no" didn't intimidate her. She grew up hearing "no" a lot. You see, Kathleen's strict father was from Italy who repeatedly told her "no." She would just rephrase what she wanted and present it again. It worked with her dad, and it worked on her customers too. During her diverse sales career, she sold copiers, computers, recruiting services and home design. No matter what she was selling, Kathleen excelled. Then, her world took an unexpected nosedive when she lost her husband, her company and more. Instead of giving up, she did the opposite. By using her God given talents and strong faith, she created a new life for herself where she inspires others who are struggling with loss of any kind, including job loss and the loss of loved ones. In 2012, Kathleen became certified as a Grief and Loss Coach. She conducts courses and holds workshops and retreats, and she has been able to help others redirect their focus from hopeless to hopeful.

Contact Information

Hoperenewedtoday.com
Info@hoperenewedtoday.com

CHAPTER THIRTEEN

My Miracle Baby
By Chelsea Collie

I am grateful for having grown up with love all around me. Although we had a large extended family, I was an only child raised by my single mother. It was just her and me most of the time. She was a nurse; she often had several days off, so we were able to go on trips and do fun things with family. We had a lot of great times in Kansas. We traveled to places like Silver Dollar City in Branson, Missouri, Disneyland in California, and we loved going snow skiing in Colorado and New Mexico. We went to a lot of museums, festivals, and concerts. It was a good life. My mom was my best friend.

Between elementary and middle school, my mom and I moved from Kansas to Austin, Texas. It was a big change, but we quickly grew to love it. My mom met a group of artists, musicians, and professionals, and it was there that she met Chris. Chris was a long-haired man who loved to read books. He was a good guy. My mom and Chris fell madly in love. Over several years, we met up with their friends, other families, and kids and just had a lot of fun. There was always music and good food.

Christmas of 1999, Mom and Chris got engaged. A few months later, in March, I turned sixteen. In June of 2000, my mom, Chris, and three friends loaded up my mom's car and started driving towards Dallas to attend a Roger Waters concert. Sadly, they never made it there. My mom's Ford Explorer had a blowout on the highway, and the vehicle smashed the concrete median and rolled several times. Chris died on the scene. My mom was ejected from the vehicle and was found unconscious. My mom was seriously injured, and she was life-flighted to a hospital in Austin, Texas. Three other passengers in the car were treated for minor injuries at the local hospital.

I went up to see my mom in her hospital room. She lay there unconscious, kept alive by the ventilator and all the machines. She was angelic, pale, and bruised. She had two black eyes and stitches above one, but she looked like she was sleeping. I could tell she was my mom, but she did not look like my mom. The sound of the breathing machine was loud. I could see her chest rising and falling as the machine pumped air in and out of her. I remember this moment vividly. It was surreal. Although it was a real-life moment, it seemed like a dream state because I had never imagined seeing something like that before.

Shortly after, a nun came in. She prayed with me over my mom, then told me that my mom had a 50/50 chance to live. She said if I just prayed, prayed harder than I ever had before, maybe she would have a chance to live. That gave me hope. So, I did. I prayed as hard as I could that whole night and into the next day. I laid next to my mom and slept with her in the hospital bed. I spent all night with her. I was holding the small Christmas portrait we had taken together the previous Christmas. Inside my mind, I talked to my mom. I confessed some things I never told her. I apologized for some things and for being a brat. I really felt like I communicated with her because I did. We had full conversations, no physical words, only the dialogue inside my head. She told me she was proud of me. I told her I needed her. I told her that she was strong and that I could not live without her. She said that I could because I was even stronger. I didn't believe it at all.

I tried to bargain with God, telling Him that if He just let my mom live, I would do whatever He wanted for the rest of my life. I felt powerless and helpless. This was way too unbelievable. I kept asking myself, is this really happening? My family from Kansas arrived the next day, and people came and visited her room in the ICU. The waiting room was packed with my family, my mom's friends, and my cousins. For whatever reason, I was still unaware of her condition, and I did not know whether or not she still had a fighting chance.

My grandma Deloris and I were called into a hospital office; we were her next of kin. There were two other people there who told us they were from the transplant team. They were walking us through some documents and said my mom had elected to be a donor. They asked about her heart, explaining it could give someone else years of life. We agreed, and they began going through the list of her other organs, one by one, asking which ones could be donated. I was confused. She was still alive. "Wait, I'm confused," I said. "Is this just in case she doesn't make it? Why are you asking us this?" The lady responded, "No, honey. Didn't anyone tell you? They completed testing this morning. It was confirmed she had no brain activity. She was declared dead at 9 a.m. this morning."

That was it. That was the moment I found out my mom was dead. She was just down the hall and still technically alive. However, no one told me she had been declared dead that morning. My heart sank. The lady explained that the doctors were just keeping her alive to complete the surgeries needed for organ donations. The confusion, the anger, the frustration rose, and I was in total disbelief that my mom's life was over. How could this have happened?

Although they could see my distress, they gave me no time to process the news. They said we still had to finish the meeting and go through everything. They continued. I wanted to scream. We said yes to donating all her organs but opted to keep her eyes. They asked about her skin. This part, beyond others, was unbelievable to me. After hanging out all day with my family by her side, finding out like this, then hearing these people ask if they could take my mom's skin, I said, "I don't think so." They went on to explain how taking some skin from her stomach and legs could help repair victims who had been severely burned. I said, "Fine." And that concluded the meeting.

I could not believe that no one had told me. There I was still hanging on to every bit of hope, praying harder than I ever had before, only to find out in a transplant meeting that my mom was brain dead and would never come back. I felt so alone. Up until that point, I had had one person I could count on no matter what. I had one person who was like my whole family, my whole support, and my whole life. I had one person who looked after me and kept me safe. And she was gone. There were people all around, yet I felt completely alone.

My mom was my whole world. Just like that, she was gone. I mustered up all my strength and decided to keep moving forward to achieve all the things we had planned on, like going to college and getting married. I wanted to make her proud. I finished high school and went on to college.

Moving Forward

I had this lust for life and determination to not take life for granted because we could die at any moment. Because of the way the car accident happened, I received a lump sum of money. I was thankful to have the money, which eliminated some worries, but the money was also a curse. It made the highs higher and the lows lower. I spent frivolously. Having the money made me question who my real friends were and who I could trust. I had some great experiences and a lot of tears and feelings of loneliness as well.

I carried on with high school and graduated. I attended college in Houston, and I never missed a party. I completed college and got my degree. However, I stayed stuck in that party mode for a long time. I was still all about fun, but I was looking for people I could truly count on. I moved a couple of times. I was always looking for something better, but I still felt stuck. After spending five years in Kansas, where things kept getting worse and worse, I eventually had enough. I moved back to Austin and started building my life back up. Piece by piece, I put my life back in order. I got my finances together, got a job, and met the man of my dreams who would become my husband.

Sean and I got married in 2016. I became an Insta-mom. My stepchildren, Tyler and Layla, are now teenagers in high school and college. I longed for a child of my own. After trying for a couple of years, I was beginning to think it was not meant to be. I recognized that as my own fear getting in the way of my dreams. So, I changed my perception. I decided if I wanted to get pregnant, I had to set the intention. At the end of 2017, I decided that by the end of 2018, I would be pregnant. In early 2018 I made a vision board and placed a picture of a positive pregnancy test on it and a picture of a big pregnant belly. I started getting ready by clearing off space in the pantry and buying little things like pacifiers. To my surprise, by August, I was pregnant! I was thrilled, happy, and so thankful. I was finally going to have the child I dreamt of and prayed for, for so long.

My Pregnancy

In the first trimester, I was tired and sick, but I got better. After that, I had a smooth pregnancy. With each check-up, the baby was healthy, and everything was progressing well. I found out I was having a little boy, and we named him Jaxon. My friends and family organized a beautiful baby shower for me around Valentine's Day with a cupid-themed "Baby Love Baby Shower." From all the tasty food and being on my feet all day, my feet swelled up that evening and pretty much stayed like that. When they got increasingly more and more swollen, I called the doctor, and they said that was normal and just to elevate my feet and rest as much as I could.

I gained 20 lbs. between weeks 32 and 34. That's 20 lbs. in two weeks. The doctor said that it was normal to be swollen, and since I had gained a total of 34 lbs. altogether, I was still right on track with where I should be weight-wise. When I went back in two weeks later for my 36-week check-up, they said that my blood pressure was high. I felt fine, but I was very swollen. The doctor told me that my blood pressure was too high. I asked if that meant that I should not go on walks. The doctor said, "No, we are going to bring a wheelchair in and take you upstairs. You are going to have this baby tonight."

I thought he was joking. I only went in for my 36-week check-up. Everything had been good up to that point with apparently "no cause for concern." I looked around at the nurses and my husband. The doctor was not joking. It was a huge shock. We were not expecting this, and we didn't even bring a hospital bag or anything. It was scary, but I did everything I could to remain calm. They diagnosed me with pre-eclampsia. They took me upstairs, started an IV, and scheduled the emergency C-section.

A Baby is Born

In the operating room, I remember just wanting to hear his cry so much, so I knew he was breathing well. He came out breach. I heard his cry, which was music to my ears. Jaxon was born on March 20th, 2019, at 6:07 p.m. He weighed 4 lbs., 7 oz., 18" long, and he came out healthy. They let me see him for only a few seconds. Sean got several pictures of our strong boy.

They took us to the recovery room. The doctor came up and let me know that he had a condition called esophageal atresia, where his throat was not connected to his stomach, and he could not swallow. The doctor informed us that he would be transported to another hospital because he needed surgery. This was where things got scary. This was one of those surreal moments. Shock after shock, and now they are taking my son to a different hospital?

When the emergency personnel came to get Jaxon, they wheeled him to my bed and let me hold him for a quick minute before they had to take him away. Here I was, suddenly, no longer pregnant, and my baby was gone.

It was a lot to handle, but I did my best to stay calm because I knew freaking out would only make things worse. Because of my high blood pressure, they started me on the magnesium treatment and monitored me throughout the next day. I continued to get even more swollen. I noticed that I was having a harder time breathing. I had shallow breathing, and when I breathed in deeply, it felt like spiderwebs in my throat. They discharged me the next day. I was so eager to leave the hospital, so I could see and hold my baby. They told me just to take it easy and take my blood pressure periodically.

My husband and I went to see Jaxon and spend time with him. I was able to do some skin-on-skin time with him. It was incredibly special. Sadly, there were so many cords everywhere. He had an IV in his arm, a suction tube in his mouth, EKG pads on his chest, and a pulse oximeter on his foot. He was starting to get jaundice and looking darker. But our sweet boy seemed comfortable, and we were happy about that. We kissed him goodbye.

We went home that night to get some rest. I was checking my blood pressure, and it was too high. I called my doctor, and he recommended I double my dose of blood pressure medication. I was so swollen that I had to keep my feet elevated. Not only were my ankles swollen, but I had pitting edema up to my thighs. I thought the swelling would go down after I had Jaxon, but it only got worse.

I felt helpless because I did not have any energy. I was supposed to be pumping milk every couple of hours, so I was up late. I was nervous about everything and just felt like something was not right. I wasn't breathing well. I had a wet feeling in my throat. When I breathed in deeply, I could feel the mucus. At one point, I thought I was having a panic attack. I woke up my husband and told him that I was having trouble breathing. He said I was just nervous, and I should try to calm down and get some sleep. I eventually fell asleep at five in the morning.

When Sean came to wake me up in the morning, I was very pale, and he said it was hard to wake me up. At this point, my breathing was much worse. We called the doctor, and they wanted me to come back to the hospital right away because I was at risk of seizure, stroke, or throwing a blood clot. They advised me to stay calm and get to the hospital. They wanted me to go to the hospital that I was discharged from, but I wanted, of course, to be at the same hospital as my baby. By the time I got to the hospital, they admitted me right away. I was happy that they admitted me into the post-partum unit, which was on the same floor as the NICU where Jaxon was.

They got the whole story of what happened, ran some tests, and hooked me up on oxygen and an IV. I experienced the worst pain of my life when they inserted a catheter into me. They started Lasix to take off all the excess fluid. Shortly after being there, we found out that there was fluid in my lungs which they diagnosed as pulmonary edema. Basically, my lungs were drowning.

Over the next twenty-four hours, they took off nineteen liters of fluid from my body. It is no wonder I couldn't breathe! Have you ever met someone who lost forty-two pounds in one day? I did. Me. I was glad to finally get some answers and feel like we had made some progress. Although yes, I felt better, in every sense of the word, I felt drained. I felt like a deflated balloon with little energy; there was nothing left in me.

Eventually, I was well enough to see Jaxon and have some extended skin-on-skin time with him. It was a great blessing to be able to walk down the hall and visit Jaxon. Because of all the trauma, my heart was affected. Tests showed that my body went into heart failure. The cardiologist attributed the heart failure to the situational stress on my body because of my high blood pressure, c-section, and all the extra fluid. He said he expected my heart to fully recover and ordered a follow-up for six months later. He prescribed medicine to keep my blood pressure down. I was in the hospital for a total of six days.

Jaxon had great medical care. I really liked his nurses. As far as all the tubes and equipment, Jaxon received all his nutrition through his pic line. He also required a suction tube to constantly clear the secretions since he was not able to swallow. Often the suction tube would get clogged, and his oxygen would start to drop, which was always scary. Either the nurse or one of us, would have to suction out the secretions. He had the pulse oximeter measuring his heart rate and oxygen and many tubes coming out everywhere. Jaxon's jaundice got worse over the coming days, so they gave him a "Billy blanket" to help normalize his bilirubin levels. This was a glowing blanket almost like a "glow-worm" plus he wore cloth glasses. With his own little tanning bed, eventually, the jaundice got better, and they were able to take the blanket off him. We got to know all the machines, alarms, cords, locations of supplies; you name it, we became experts of care for Jaxon. The nurses and doctors changed constantly, and we were the only ones who knew what worked best for Jaxon specifically.

I liked being in the hospital with Jaxon since they let me go see him whenever I wanted. After I was discharged, it was much more difficult to be there, having to drive in from thirty miles away. The best thing in the world was that the hospital had a webcam for the parents to login and look at their child when they could not be there. This gave us so much peace.

About ten days after Jaxon was born, they said it was time to place the feeding tube, and Jaxon had to undergo surgery to place a g-button in his stomach. Sean's mom was a constant at the hospital, and we all met before surgery. We walked down the long hall and had to kiss him goodbye at the elevator when they took him down to the operating room. That was a very scary walk. It was one we would have to do often. It is always nerve-wracking when your child has to go under anesthesia. In these tough moments when it seemed like everyone was nervous, Jaxon was always the calmest one.

In total, Jaxon was in the NICU for 110 days. He was the oldest one there. The nurses loved him so much. His smile would make their day. He was such a happy boy. Even through all the tough times, after yet another poke, a couple of seconds later he would be smiling again. It is hard to remember how sick he really was because he always seemed like he was either okay or he was going to be okay. He took everything in stride. When I look back at the pictures and videos, I think. "Wow, was it really that bad?" Yes, it was tough for a while. This short synopsis does not begin to cover our experience in the NICU. Jaxon had to undergo four major surgeries, three of which were back-to-back, three weeks in a row. These three surgeries ultimately connected his esophagus so he could swallow from mouth to stomach.

My support with Sean was invaluable because we were united, and we became even stronger together. We compensated for each other. When I was having a weak moment, he was strong. When he was having a weak moment, I was strong. I felt like we allowed each other to be where we were at. We did our best to communicate with the hospital staff and relay the information to each other. This time was stressful enough, and we supported each other through it.

What I Learned

Through the hardship, I have learned that we find out who we truly are in times of struggle. We find our true character. When times get tough, we get going. We find out who our true supporters are as well. During these tough times, I had to remind myself that because I knew that this was only temporary, Jaxon would fully recover and live a full life. I had to remind myself that no matter if he were in the NICU for a few weeks or for several months, I knew that we would eventually get through it, and he would be 100% okay. Even in his "sickness," he was strong. Even though we had a constant battle for a long time with secretions in his throat, he was always healthy. He had a solid heart, fully functioning organs, he was still learning and developing through all of it, and above all, he was strong.

Another key to progress during a challenge was to remind myself to practice gratitude. We were going through major challenges. At the same time, I was grateful to have a happy, beautiful baby boy. I was so thankful to have this incredible soul, this incredible warrior who taught us to never give up. He never stopped fighting, not for a second. With every horrendous procedure, every single IV, shot, swallow study, and every test, he was smiling a minute later. The entire NICU stay, he was truly an inspiration. Sometimes we had to borrow his determination and strength to carry on.

Also, many esophageal atresia babies have other health conditions like seizures or require the children to be fed fully with the feeding tube, be in a wheelchair, or on oxygen. We are so thankful that his condition was contained to just his esophagus.

During this time, I learned that it was important to show up. And sometimes, showing up meant going home or even staying home. I was in that NICU more than any other parent, and I was just so thankful that I could be there with him. I don't know if I could have gotten through it if I had to go to work every day. However, there were times when I felt guilty because I could not be there 24/7. In those times, I had to remind myself that I had to take care of myself too. Several times the nurses kindly told me that the best thing I could do was to go home and get some sleep. I knew I had to trust the process because Jaxon was always protected and cared for. I worked with the hospital staff to schedule the most supportive nurses for Jaxon each shift. They loved him and took care of him like he was their own. Often, I had to remind myself that I could not give him the level of care at home that the NICU could provide, so I needed to be patient. They had the equipment, the staff, the doctors, and the operating room if necessary. He was very safe, and I was confident in his care and that he was well tended to. If I ever had any doubt, I could log in to the webcam or call at any time to check on him.

Throughout each day in the NICU, it became apparent that the bond between Jaxon and me, the bond between mother and baby, was so strong. He was in synchronicity with me in real time. If I didn't let myself get worried or upset, I knew that he was going to be okay. If I needed him to be okay, I had to be okay. If he was upset and crying and needed to calm down, I had to calm down. If the energy was getting tense and he needed to breathe to get his oxygen back up, I took a deep breath and focused on my breathing, and he would breathe and get his oxygen back up.

Even on the scary long walks down the hall to say goodbye at the elevator. I felt good saying goodbye when they took him down for a procedure because I knew he was going to be okay. Because he had to be okay, and for that to happen, I had to be okay. The bond is strong. Our energy was instantaneously connected. Energy is real; it is more real than anything else we are surrounded by. That feeling of okay, that deep knowing, drove us all to the positive outcome.

If you are going through a hard time, do not prepare for the worst-case scenario. Focus on the best-case scenario. Prepare and expect the best, and even if that doesn't happen, be thankful for progress. Focus on what you want and recognize progress at every stage.

I struggled so many times in my life, and I kept searching for the answer outside of myself, only to find that I had the answer all along. Remember to look within. It is important to identify your support system and lean on them but pray for what you want and have faith that you will receive that. Know that these challenges, although uncomfortable, are only temporary and, "this too shall pass."

If you feel like you are powerless in a situation, recognize your power, and put the focus on that. If you are having trouble finding your power, identify your limiting beliefs. Underneath every limiting belief is a loving truth. Redefine that situation and choose to reframe the belief with the loving truth. Find the strength inside you and use that strength, that power to propel you through any challenge. You are stronger than you think you are.

At the time of this writing, Jaxon has successfully conquered eleven procedures and three hospital stays, besides the NICU. He is a happy, healthy toddler who is regularly eating and drinking by mouth. He is still inspiring mom, dad, and the whole family. He is keeping us busy and running around like crazy. Life is crazy and good. I would not have it any other way.

About the Author

Chelsea Collie is an Empowerment Specialist, Inspirational Speaker, Real Estate Investor & Author. Chelsea is the Founder & CEO of Spread Love Speak Life whose vision is to elevate the world by the power of love.

Chelsea's book, Be a Life Breather: Transform your Vision into Reality combines Chelsea's powerful story, an inspiring message, along with a workbook that will serve as a roadmap for readers to achieve their wildest dreams. Her mission is to empower 10,000 women and moms to Skyrocket to Success by 2030.

Having had a traumatic experience at the age of 16, Chelsea had the option of letting loss and heartbreak rule her destiny or find the power to rise above. She chose to let her experience propel her forward in her mission of helping and inspiring others.

Chelsea currently resides in Austin, Texas with her husband, children, and pets. Chelsea's hobbies include live music, attending personal growth events, and spending time with friends. She and her husband enjoy investing in real estate and renovating properties.

She has become unstoppable and so can you.

Contact Information

Chelsea @spreadlovespeaklife.com

CHAPTER FOURTEEN

When Our Outsides Don't Match Our Insides

By Sheryl Dearth-Arvizu

I was lying in a hospital bed in a Colorado emergency room when the door opened, and a physician walked into the room. She greeted me and flipped through pages on a clipboard. She then said, "I'm sorry, I have the wrong room." About 10 minutes later she returned. She looked at me quizzically and asked, "Are you Sheryl?" The medical conditions and medications listed on her chart were apparently correct. When I said yes, she said, "I am sorry, when I came into the room and looked at your chart and then at you, I thought I had the wrong room. You look much healthier and younger than what I was expecting based on your medical history."

Bloodwork and a scan confirmed I had appendicitis, and I was taken to surgery to have my appendix removed. After I recovered, her words remained in my mind. Her assessment was right, and it continues today. I do look healthier on the outside than I am on the inside.

My childhood was anything but normal. My parents owned a nightclub, so they worked totally different hours than my friends' parents. I started dance lessons at the age of 4. By age 5, I earned a solo performance in our dance recital. When I was 7, my dance teacher recommended that my mom enroll me into gymnastics classes at the training center in town. I caught on fast. In the first week of classes, an assistant coach grabbed me out of class and took me over to one of the low beams. Within a few minutes, she taught me how to do a no-handed cartwheel on the beam. With excitement, she brought the head coach over and had me show him what I had learned. On the drive home, Mom informed me that the head coach had promoted me, and I was now a member of the C team.

The girls on the A team competed nationally and internationally. The B team competed regionally and were on an intermediate level. The C team competed at the beginner level, which involved travel to neighboring states. The head coach of the gymnastics center turned out to be Dick Mulvahill, The U.S. Women's Gymnastics Team's head coach. Several girls from our gym had made the national and Olympic teams.

At the age of 7, I began training for the Olympics. A normal day consisted of school followed by dance class and then over to the gym to train. I would get home most nights after my family had finished dinner and would eat a plate of reheated food, do my homework, go to sleep, and repeat.

By age 8, I was traveling to other states to compete. It was then I noticed I became sick more often than my teammates and school friends. If I walked outside in the winter without a hat and scarf, I was sure to develop swollen glands in my neck, a fever, and a sore throat that lasted for days. I suffered from motion sickness, which made long car rides to other states miserable. When I stayed in hotel rooms with the other girls, they all quickly fell to sleep. I would lie there for hours, unable to sleep.

As I started to compete at a higher level, the judges told my coach that I needed to gain a little weight. Stop and think about that. When all my teammates were trying to keep weight off, my coach was urging me to gain weight. When traveling we would stop for lunch or dinner. My coach would make sure I ate my food then ordered my dessert and made sure I ate it all.

When our coach instructed us to run to "warm up," I was always at the back of the pack. When I finished my floor routine, I would be more out of breath than my teammates. I had normal childhood illnesses like chicken pox, the stomach flu, influenza, and strep throat. In eighth grade I fell ill with scarlet fever, which was not as common.

As a kid, I always seemed to be having accidents that would require a trip to the emergency room. Falling off my bicycle, cutting my foot, burning my leg on my minibike all required trips to the ER. The physician walked into the room and commented, "Oh no, not you again, Sheryl. What did you do this time?"

In the fourth grade, I broke my ankle doing a dismount off the bars and was sent home. When the radiologist read the x-ray, they found I was walking on a broken ankle for a day before I returned to the hospital to get a cast. I recovered and four weeks later returned to the gym with minimal disruption to my training except that my ankle was weaker, and I would frequently re-sprain it. I continued training and added physical therapy into my routine. As I sat doing homework, I picked marbles up out of a pie pan using my toes and moved my ankle into a position to drop them into another pie pan. Repeat.

When I was 12 and the youngest member of the A team, I traveled to Europe to compete. In the host homes where we stayed, I remember how the mom would always try to get me to eat. In Germany, Switzerland, and Austria the comments were always, "You are so skinny, you need to put some meat on your bones." Throughout my junior high years, I continued to miss more practice than my teammates and more school than my classmates. What I didn't know then was that extensive physical training and little sleep was taking its toll on my tired body. My young body, mottled with black-and-blue bruises and racked with sore muscles, continued each day to absorb the abuse that I unknowingly was heaping onto myself. Because I so often missed school and training days, I had to push all the harder to catch up.

In my junior year of high school, I broke my thumb during a game of flag football in PE class. Back in the 70s our school system did not allow exclusion from physical education for students training in club sports. School athletes could sit out of PE, but as a club athlete, if I had a meet that started at 3 p.m., I still had to participate in gym class.

That thumb injury changed the trajectory of my gymnastics career. I went to the gym with a brace on my left hand and worked out the best I could to prepare for competition. The brace came off one week before the first competition of our season. With my thumb healed, I pushed to catch up to be prepared for our first meet. The day of the competition, everything seemed fine. I did well, not great, but my coach was encouraging.

I returned to the gym two days later to reset and focus on training for our next competition. Something was wrong. Every time I would jump, tumble, run, or land a dismount, I had a horrible pinching pain on both of my hip bones. Another trip to the hospital.

The doctor explained that the cartilage had separated from the top of my hip bones, which sometimes afflicted distance runners. He assumed the injury occurred because I had pushed to get ready to compete. Treatment was to discontinue training for eight weeks and then slowly return to my normal training. Those were exceedingly difficult weeks for me. I was so used to being active. I remember standing on my hands in the family room and my father jokingly saying, "Aren't you getting tired of that, isn't there something else you can go do?"

I honestly did not know what to do with my time. This would become a recurring theme in my life. My homework was complete. Household chores done. I had lived such a high-paced life that I had no idea what to do with free time. I woke up during the sixth week of my rest/recovery with horrible back pain. Now what?

Once again, more x-rays. What these x-rays showed was that my spine had shifted. I was diagnosed with scoliosis, my curve measured at 14 percent. The orthopedic doctor put my x-rays up on the screen to show my mother and me. He explained the scoliosis and then told me that there was no reason I should be having back pain. He looked at me and asked, "Are you trying to get out of going to school?"

WHAT???

I was a gymnast. I was tough. I was taught during training that if you fall and get hurt, you get back up and do it again and again and again. For him to say that was confusing to me. I knew pain and I knew how to "get up and do it again" despite the pain. If I said it hurt, IT HURT. It was emotionally crushing. I know now that I felt so helpless because of his demeaning words and attitude.

In those days, we did not have the internet to double-check our diagnosis or connect with others who might have been experiencing similar issues. It was not common for a patient to question a doctors' opinion. That was my first and most memorable encounter with a physician that told me that the tests and their opinion did not support what I was feeling, experiencing, and conveying to them. There would be more interactions with health care providers to come, and each interaction left me more discouraged.

Forty years later, I still have moderate pain in my back. The diagnosis now is a pinched nerve causing a constant muscle spasm. I have had steroid injections into the knot, have taken muscle relaxers and participated in physical therapy. The adult me would like to tell that physician, "How dare you tell me I should not be having pain. If you don't know the cause of my pain, don't dismiss me, refer me to someone who can help!"

I returned to training and fought through the back pain "that didn't exist." I started rehab to strengthen my back muscles that had weakened during my recent injuries. My schedule now became school, rehab, gym, dinner, homework (sometimes I wouldn't finish until midnight or 1 a.m.). I would try to sleep, get up, and repeat. I was in pain, exhausted, and burnt out. I kept asking myself, why should I continue to put myself through the pain and the stress? I eventually stepped out of gymnastics and moved forward. I was still in pain but every day I wondered if I should return and start training again. Gymnastics had been "my life." I constantly questioned my decision and then a political decision occurred.

The 1980 Summer Olympic Games were held in Moscow, Russia. But the United States boycotted to protest the 1979 invasion of Afghanistan. Had I continued to train through the pain and by some miracle made the Olympic team, I would not have been able to participate. The many athletes who had spent their young lives training for the Olympics only to have their dream snatched away were heartbroken. Ironically, for me, it became a solace, a confirmation that I had made the right decision.

I had changed my focus. I joined the cheerleading squad my senior year of high school and became the tumbling tiger mascot. I ran for and became senior class president. I participated in choir and the spring musical. My senior year of high school was the first year that my life began to seem normal.

But then, I missed almost the whole last month of school with an odd infection. My throat was covered with a white coating; my uvula was swollen so large that I had to lean forward to breathe. The doctors could not figure out what was wrong. Tests for mononucleosis and strep came back negative.

I returned to school after all the other seniors were done with class. The juniors and sophomores still had two days of class left before summer break. On senior "skip day" I remember standing in senior hall alone, exhausted and hoping just to pass the finals and get good enough grades on the homework I had just turned in to graduate. I was an A student, and my new goal was to pass and graduate!

I started college and continued to experience more severe and longer-lasting respiratory illnesses. While it was nothing serious, I was always "catching something." I finished my associate degree and entered nursing school. I worked as a cocktail waitress in my parents' bar to help pay for my school and earn a little spending money. I would get home from work at around 2 or 3 a.m. and then study. On the nights before clinicals, I would finish patient-care plans before the ritual of trying to sleep. My mornings at the hospital started at 6 a.m. I remember taking caffeine tablets before going to bed just to make sure I could get out of bed when the alarm rang two or three hours later. I made it through college with minor health issues, but the physical and emotional stress was accumulating.

During this time, my 29-year-old uncle was diagnosed with ALS. He passed away a year later. In the following 12 months, I attended the funerals of four additional family members. I stuffed the emotional stress inside and pushed forward. I took a full-time job as a home health care nurse and office assistant, worked part-time at a long-term care pediatric facility, coached gymnastics, and waited tables at my parents' club. The pace felt comfortable to me. The physical stress was still taking its toll, but I didn't know how to recognize it.

I married at the age of 23 and by the time I turned 28 I had a beautiful baby girl, a sweet 1-year old son, and an amazing 2-year-old daughter. Yes, three kids, all under the age of 3.

My marriage was stressful. My mother-in-law was a narcissistic nightmare. My husband was selfish and most of the work with our children and at home fell on my shoulders. That is a separate book!

Between pregnancies I worked at my parents' bar because waiting tables provided more income than working as a licensed nurse. I wanted to finish my bachelor's degree, so I applied and completed my first class right before the birth of my third child. I had planned to take a semester off to take care of my three little babies, then return to school. What came next would shatter me to the core and change the rest of my life in a way I could never have imagined.

I became a member of a club that I did not want to belong to. My pain was surreal, but I didn't have time for crying all day and night. I could not stay in bed and pull the covers over my head. I had to get up, put a smile on my face and take care of the three most precious things in my life. How do you tell a 2-, 3- and 4-year-old that their grandpa has passed away? He was not a perfect man, but he was my "perfect father!"

My husband and I had been unpacking all day. It was the first day moving into our new home. I was exhausted. I called my father to check in. He was diabetic and was home after recovering from a major heart attack and awaiting surgery. I asked if he would like me to come over and stay until my mom got home from the bar.

He said, "Of course not, I am fine. You take care of your little ones."
I said, "I love you, Dad."
He said, "I love you, too."
I continued, "Dad, call if you need anything."
He said, "Will do. I will talk to you tomorrow!"
I had him write down my new phone number (we still had landlines back then).
My final words to him were, "Talk to you tomorrow, Dad!"

The phone ringing woke me up. I jumped out of bed, dazed. I couldn't find the phone. It stopped ringing. Anxiety hit me hard; a phone ringing in the middle of the night means something is wrong.

I kept rummaging in the dark, desperately trying to find the phone. It was my mom on the other end, and she was screaming, "Sheryl, he did it again. I called 911 and the paramedics are here. Meet us at the ER."

My parents lived about seven minutes from the ER. I hung up and rushed to move boxes to find clothes to put on. I couldn't find my keys and my husband awoke yelling, "What the heck!"

I said something has happened to Dad and I can't find the keys. He handed me the keys to his manual transmission vehicle. Crap. It had been years since I drove with a clutch.

I ran out. I drove the 20 minutes to the ER. I parked in front and ran inside. I obviously looked panicked as the security guard took my keys and said he would park the vehicle for me. He conveyed that they had communicated with the paramedics and my father would be transported shortly. I paced back-and-forth, stuffing the anxiety inside. I said to myself, "Be strong, don't cry, you need to be the strong one!" I paced, and then I saw the ambulance back in.

They rushed my father past me still doing CPR. I bit my lips as I saw my mother and sisters run in. Just as quickly someone's hand was on my mother's elbow and they were directing us to a door that they unlocked. We were escorted inside a private room and asked if there was anything we needed. My heart sank. I knew this was the type of room where hospital workers took the loved ones of critically ill patients. I told myself, "Don't you dare cry. Your mom and sisters need you to be strong." I stuffed it in as the pressure built higher and the ache inside got stronger.

My father passed. Like a scene from TV, the doctor walked out with the nurse and gave us the "we tried everything speech."

I do believe they tried everything. Then the nurse mistakenly asked my mother to sign a form so my father could be an organ donor. The look on my mom's face as the reality set in still haunts me as much as the guttural scream, she let out the morning she received the call that her little brother had passed. I had to step in and ask the nurse if my fathers' arteries and veins were not viable for a heart transplant, does he qualify as a donor? My baby sister threw herself on the floor sobbing and my older sister stood in shock. I continued to tell myself, "Be strong, stuff it in." I needed to call Uncle Woody and my brother who was living in Colorado.

I arrived back home in a daze. My husband came charging in from the garage, yelling at me, wanting to know where "something!" was. He was aware that my father had passed; I had called him from the ER with the news. He stomped his foot in anger and yelled, "This is the worst day of my life."

I held back the tears.

Days passed. I continued to stuff in the hurt, and the loss, and the anger. My life continued to be filled with stress and too little sleep. My father was in the process of selling his business when he passed. My kids were little. I was doing after-school day care. I went back to working evenings for my mother, bartending as she continued to try to sell the business. I would make dinner, grab a bite of food as my family sat down to eat, and I returned home at about 2 a.m. I would clean up the dishes left on the table and try to get some rest before my three little ones woke up. I continued working toward my bachelors' degree, taking classes at night and on weekends. The pace was exhausting, but it felt comfortable.

Spring came and the river behind our new home started overflowing. All the neighbors jumped in and started sandbagging behind our house and all of the other homes that backed up to the river. At about 9 p.m. my husband told me he was going to bed because he had to work in the morning.

My kids were safe at my grandmother's place, so I continued sandbagging with the men in the neighborhood until 5 a.m., when it seemed safe to try to get some rest. The river retreated and two nights later, I was back at work, bartending with my sister.

Toward the end of the night, I walked over to her and said, "Something is not right. I feel like I am going to pass out."

I rested against a support beam and when I could no longer stand, I slid down into a sitting position. I could not lift my head. My sister and mom drove me to the ER. My blood pressure was low, and I was shivering, but I didn't have a temperature. After several hours lying there, breathing with an oxygen mask and covered with heated blankets, my vitals stabilized. The diagnosis was that I probably came into contact with a virus while sandbagging, and I was told to go home and rest.

The next morning and for several days I ached all over. They must have been right, some strange virus. Two weeks later, I was almost back to normal. I was getting the kids ready for bed, and I suddenly felt like I was going to pass out. I was very nauseous and again went to the floor. I couldn't stand up.

My husband started yelling at me, "What the hell is wrong now?" With tears in my eyes, I called my sister. She made the 20-minute drive to my home. She and my husband had to carry me to the car. This time at the ER when they checked my blood pressure it was

56/42, dangerously low. I was immediately taken into a trauma room. The nurse asked what I had eaten that day. I couldn't remember specifically what I ate, but I do know I was eating over twice as much as my husband in a day. When I told her, she asked if I had thrown it up, I looked very thin. I had not thrown up. I had been thin since I could remember. The doctor ordered a blood-gas and a breathing treatment. My CO_2 was below normal, and as a result, my blood pressure dropped. He diagnosed me with asthma.

After a few hours, my vitals were normal, and I returned home with a follow-up appointment scheduled with my internal-medicine physician. During that visit, my physician prescribed albuterol "an inhaler/bronchodilator," along with antihistamine and a nasal steroid. She confirmed the ER doctor's diagnosis of asthma. It made sense. All those years training as hard as I had, I could never finish running one mile without walking part of it. I had an answer. I had asthma.

I took my medicines as prescribed, but something was wrong. When I used the inhaler my heart rate shot up to 160 at rest. I was so shaky from head-to-toe that when I tried to walk, I shook all over. I returned to my physician. She explained some patients had a hyper response to albuterol and prescribed a different type of bronchodilator. I continued to have symptoms. I continued to see my physician. During one of my visits, she patted me on the shoulder and said, "Oh honey, don't worry. You are a young mom with little kids, everything is fine." Everything was not fine. I was still underweight even though I was consuming approximately 9,000-12,000 calories a day. I did not gain weight.

Two years later, I graduated with my bachelor's degree with straight As and secured a job as a pharmaceutical sales representative for a top company. All the work was worth it. A few months into the job, during a routine physical, I found out I needed to have a hysterectomy. The procedure went well. I returned home to rest. The only problem was I had to be in New Jersey in four weeks to train on a new product I would be promoting. My recovery time turned into study time.

I left four weeks after major surgery to attend the two-week training. I ignored my pain; I pushed beyond the exhaustion and did what I had been trained to do: perform no matter what. Get up, dust myself off and do it again! I returned home to my job and family responsibilities and still did not feel OK. This continued for a couple of years.

While attending an educational event, an endocrinologist approached me and said, "I never know when I should say anything or not, but have you ever had your thyroid checked; you look "Gravesy." Of the health care providers sitting by me, one I had known since childhood replied, "OMG, I think you are right. I never noticed."

I was urged to have my bloodwork done. I would, but my first priority was to make sure my kids had everything they needed. I had a job to do and a house to take care of and I would get my bloodwork done at my next physical. Even though I had heard the saying, "Put your oxygen mask on first, then help those next to you" I still was not taking care of me. A couple of months after that educational event I showed up at one of the provider's offices for a work appointment. The nurse practitioner commented, "Wow, you look bad. The circles under your eyes are really dark. Have you had your blood checked?" Of course, I had not. She ordered blood work immediately. She called me later that day with the results. I was extremely hyperthyroid, and she recommended I see my physician as soon as possible. I decided at that point to change my primary caregiver. I knew something was wrong and had been placated and told not to worry more than once. It was time for a change.

I sought care from a highly recommended internal-medicine physician who worked with a different health care system in town. He agreed with the probable diagnosis of Graves Disease and I was then treated by an endocrinologist. It took a while to get my condition under control. I ingested radioactive iodine and had to stay several feet away from my kids for days. I was not allowed to touch them or their food. During that process I was told I did not respond normally to the medication. It was not the last time I would hear that comment in some form or another. I continued, enjoying my job and my children. My thyroid was finally under control. But for the first time in my life, I had to watch everything I ate. My once overactive metabolism had come to a medically induced halt. Instead of making sure I had eaten enough calories during the day, often eating when not hungry, I now had to start making sure I did not eat too many calories.

As I went through treatment for my thyroid condition, I learned to listen to my body. On a follow up visit to my endocrinologist, she ordered my blood to be drawn to check my body's thyroid levels.

She said, "I can tell by looking at you that you are now very hypothyroid. I don't want you to wait until the bloodwork comes back. Start taking your Synthroid (thyroid replacement hormone) now." I asked if she was sure, as I was still feeling "hyperthyroid." She said "yes" and I did as instructed. I took a dose of Synthroid and continued with my job, driving an hour south to attend work appointments with physicians. I started not feeling well and at about 3 p.m. my resting heart rate increased to 165. I could feel my heart flopping in my chest. I called my endocrinologist's office where I spoke with the nurse and told her how I was feeling.

She said, "Well, that doesn't make any sense. You are probably just really stressed."
I said, "Will you please have the doctor call me?"
I drove to a gas station and purchased a 7-up to drink.

At this point, I was unable to drive. I was lightheaded and my heart was pounding. After resting in my car for about an hour, I drove back home and decided not to take any more Synthroid until my blood results came back.

Two days later, I received a call from my physician. She said "Please stop taking the Synthroid. I was wrong, your levels are still really high." I had stopped taking it after one dose. From there on out, I approached my health care differently. I would now question the decisions of my physicians and the instructions they gave me.

I continued the relentless pace for a few more years. I won sales awards and completed management training. At age 38, something was wrong again. We had just moved again, out into the country on seven acres in central Illinois. Winter had set in. I could hear the cold wind hitting the side of the house as I tried to fall asleep. I woke up for several mornings in a row with swollen feet. Every bone in my feet hurt. It was painful just to walk to the bathroom. The pain would go away as the day progressed. Surely it was from the winter cold. In just four weeks, it went away as quickly as it had arrived. So, it was nothing.

My job, at the time, required a lot of driving including a trip from Central Illinois to the south suburbs of Chicago at least two days a week. On the long drive home, I started feeling an uncomfortable pressure inside my knees. I couldn't explain it. I thought maybe it was all the hours driving in the car. That pain lasted for about four weeks, then it was gone. I had just changed company vehicles from a coupe to an SUV and was now sitting in a different position. I assumed that was the cause. But in the back of my mind, I knew something was going on. I started learning to play golf that summer. I must admit I hit the ground with the end of the club way more often than I hit the ball. As a result, my elbows and wrists started hurting. Not like they did when I was training as an athlete; this pain was different. Something was wrong. Or was it? I told my next-door neighbor and best friend that something was not right.

She gave me a hard time saying, "You always think something is wrong."

I said, "Yes! And how many times am I right? I need to go have it checked."

She kind of blew off my concerns.

The lesson I was learning was that if you look fine on the outside, you might not be fine on the inside. The next morning, I woke up to find my right arm swollen, cold and slightly purple from my shoulder to my fingertips. I wondered if it was a blood clot blocking my circulation. I called my neighbor as she was good friends with my primary care physician. The doctor would fit me in as soon as I got there. I asked my friend to go along with me. My physician asked me what I thought it was. I had been on the internet and I had three thoughts: Lyme Disease, Lupus, or Rheumatoid Arthritis (RA). My doctor agreed and ordered blood tests and hoped it was not Scleroderma. He shared that what was happening was serious and that I should rest. He referred me to a rheumatologist.

At my doctor's appointment, my hands were so swollen that I had difficulty dressing myself and styling my hair. My feet were swollen and every joint in my feet hurt too badly to fit into tennis shoes. I could only wear sandals. My elbows and wrists were swollen, red, warm, and painful and I was diagnosed with RA. The disease was no longer playing around, it wasn't teasing my feet or elbows. It was full blown. I was 38 years old and faced with an unknown future. How long would I be able to physically take care of myself, let alone my family? How long would I be able to work? I decided on the drive home that this illness was not going to control me, that I was going to control it! I was glad it was me and not one of my children and it was not fatal. I could do this!

I found any information I could about RA and educated myself. I followed my doctor's orders and was able to go into remission thanks to a cocktail of medications. What I learned about autoimmune illnesses—I had now been diagnosed with three of them—is that they usually "come in threes." The direct cause for autoimmune illnesses is unknown. Was there a genetic predisposition? It turns out almost all patients presenting with an autoimmune illness experienced severe stress prior to their diagnosis. That was one box I could check. I had endured more physical and mental stress then most others I knew.

It was obvious that I needed to learn how to reduce my stress level. My husband was offered a job in Colorado and I agreed to move. I wasn't sure at that time how severe my RA would become. Would I have a mild illness or end up disabled? I was determined to live a full life while I could. I learned to ski and have been white-water rafting. I have grabbed life by the horns and try to do as much as I can.

Over the next several years, I continued my career in pharmaceuticals. The drive and mental conditioning I had learned as a young child served me well in the industry. I would continue to be a top performer despite suffering more health issues. I had learned at this point in my career to keep my illness to myself for internal and external reasons. For me, I did not want to be perceived as someone who could not do the job. I was internally motivated to perform despite my health. I went to great lengths to hide my illnesses. I took a promotion to a high-travel position. I challenged myself with rotations into the corporate office. At one point I was commuting to Boston while living in Denver and covering the Pacific Northwest as my sales territory. There were crazy hours, jumping time zones, continual lack of sleep, and high pressure to perform in a competitive industry. I am sure my health suffered through all this determination to achieve success and prove myself to be highly capable.

In my mid-forties, things changed. I could no longer go without sleep, push myself beyond what was normal, and expect my body to continue to go along. My body started "screaming" at me to slow down and listen. I could no longer put everyone else's mask on while I was starved for oxygen. My body simply would not allow it any longer.

Did I completely ignore my health all those years? No. I questioned physicians when they told me that I was OK. I now seek a second opinion if needed. I do my own research on my concerns using reputable resources. I come prepared to my doctor's appointments with questions. I write down my symptoms when they occur, so I don't forget. I have learned to be my own health advocate. For me, the process is ongoing. Calming my internal overachiever behavior has been difficult. It has been a process of making positive decisions including healthier eating and exercise. When life gets busy and old habits creep back in, my body will not so kindly remind me. When I realize that I am starting to fall into old patterns, I quickly self-correct. I now continually incorporate new activities into my life that are good for my physical and mental health. These days I try to keep my oxygen mask on. It is true, it is so much easier and less taxing to help others when you have taken care of yourself first.

I encourage people to educate themselves, ask questions, seek second opinions, and be your own advocate to receive the best treatment possible! Find alternative approaches to how you live your life to make it the best possible life. You will undoubtedly have to make compromises but choose wisely. Prioritize what is most important and let the rest go.

About the Author

Sheryl is currently serving as a Board Director for the New Mexico Bioscience Authority. She has more than two decades experience in the pharmaceutical industry and has worked for several prominent corporations including Bayer Health Care, Gilead Sciences, Genentech, Novartis, and Vertex. She has been a major contributor to the launch of over 15 innovative life changing medications. Early in her career she worked in sales for Hoffman La Roche/Genentech where she launched the popular drug Tamiflu. Her role included educating physicians and other health care professionals on the pivotal clinical trials and appropriate use of Tamiflu. She also worked as a Respiratory Specialist for Novartis and Schering-Plough educating health care providers on various Asthma and COPD products. She has extensive experience in the rare, ultra-rare and orphan disease space including diseases such as Pulmonary Hypertension, Cystic Fibrosis, LAL-D (Lysosomal Acid Lipase Deficiency) and Myasthenia Gravis. While working at Vertex Pharmaceuticals she launched Kalydeco (the first genetic potentiator) whose launch, at the time, was recognized by several entities as the most successful pharmaceutical launch in the history of the industry.

She has held various roles in the industry including, Sales, Sales Training, Sales Management, Marketing and Business Analytics. She has won several awards for her Sales performance for the successful launch of many products and other awards for her contributions in various areas of the industry including sales training and marketing. Before working in Pharmaceuticals, she worked as a pediatric and home health care nurse. She received her nursing degree from Parkland college and a B.O.T.B.A (Board of Trusties Bachelor of Arts) from Eastern Illinois University. She is currently finishing her master's in business administration.

Contact Information

sherylkarvizu@gmail.com

Discovering My Power and Purpose in a Jail Cell

By Michelle Faust

On Valentine's Day, 2020. we were on vacation in New Orleans just before Mardi Gras. My husband, Dean, and I decided to spend a day in the French Quarter. Rather than a formal evening dinner celebration, we noshed our way through the day planning to go back to our vacation rental early and enjoy a nice bottle of wine.

We started at "The Port of Call," which serves up a Bloody Mary that is a meal. It is full of green beans, olives, pearl onions, celery, and the right amount of kick. Just walking the French Quarter is a treat with all its stately Victorian buildings and unique shops. It was a beautiful day and we felt alive and happy to be back in one of our favorite places. We capped off the day with charbroiled oysters at "Acme Seafood House." These oysters will invade your dreams— they are that good. Dean made plans to go back the next day to catch up with a server he had befriended the last time we visited. We then went next door for a few games of pool before leaving the French Quarter.

Around 7:30 p.m., I attempted to contact a Lyft or Uber driver, but both my Lyft and Uber apps on my phone were not working. So, instead, we decided to take a taxi. The restaurant manager called up a taxi. It was a minivan with no outside graphics to indicate it was a taxi. That should have been a red flag. The driver had a heavy

Asian accent and was difficult to understand. About a mile into the ride, I saw on the meter a charge of $35. As we were only going about seven miles and a typical Uber fare would be $10, I asked about it, and he said it was a flat rate. I told him he was taking advantage of us because we were tourists. He seemed irritated and responded, but I could not understand what he was saying.

When we arrived at our rental, Dean got out as I was paying the fare. I gave the driver $20 and said that was all I was willing to pay. In truth, it was not even about the money; it was the way he treated us and how he was trying to take advantage of us. When he requested I pay the remaining balance by credit card, I refused and he threw the $20 back at me and said he was going to call the cops. I said, "Fine because I feel like I've just been robbed." I did not feel threatened because I believe in law enforcement being committed to finding peaceful solutions. That is not so in St. Bernard Parish.

I heard a knock on the door. When I opened it, I saw several officers in the background. The officer at the door was big, burly, and bald. He had a tough guy stance about him and a cowboy attitude. He asked what happened and if I was willing to pay the driver. Communication was challenging at this point because there was a lot of outside noise. I did not realize this was our first and last chance at clearing this up. I said, "I'm having a really hard time agreeing to that because I feel I am being taken advantage of." Looking back, I realize I should have just paid the bill, but this was not a typical week for me, and I was not thinking clearly.

CHAPTER FIFTEEN

Just three days before our trip, my ex-husband died, and I had been dealing with my two daughter's grief. This took me out of my routine and added significant stress to an already stressful week. Consequently, I was not taking care of myself or taking my depression meds regularly. So, when the officer asked if my husband was inside the house, I said, "Yes, he's in the kitchen." I was relieved because I knew Dean would be the voice of reason when I did not feel capable.

Dean didn't have a chance to explain anything as the officer told him he was under arrest. Being of small stature, Dean did not argue and immediately said he would not resist and would go peacefully with them. As he said that, he placed his palm on his chest, like an honorable gesture. Unknown to him, in the criminal word, that signifies resistance. They immediately cuffed his left wrist and wrenched his arthritic arm (still placed on his chest) around his back to cuff, then forcibly removed him from the kitchen.

Meanwhile, we both repeatedly stated we would pay the driver, but this peaceful solution was no longer an option. As I watched this happen in disbelief, another officer was saying something about my shoes. I could only focus on my husband's mistreatment, so I didn't clearly understand he was telling me to put on my shoes. The next thing I know, he slaps cuffs on me and starts to push me towards the door and down the porch steps. I was confused and frightened.

The officer behind me was giving me commands which I could not follow. For those of you who know me or have read my story in The Lemonade Stand, you know I have a severe hearing loss and depend on reading lips to aid in understanding what someone is saying. I was barefoot and my vertigo was triggered causing me to pull away. In hindsight, I can see how that could be interpreted as resistance, but it was 100% due to my health and disability. Before being shoved into the car, the officer noticed the left handcuff was off my wrist. It fell off my wrist because he put it on too loose. He was angry and put them back on, telling me not to do that again. While in the police car, I noticed he put the left cuff on loosely again. I could not believe that a responsible, trained officer would do that twice, so I let my wrist easily slip out again. I did not do it with an intent to escape, rather as a statement that maybe the officer should be held accountable. Those loose handcuffs bought me two felonies for simple attempted escape and intent to escape.

Before entering the jail, the cops shoved us against the wall with our backs to them. This was the only time Dean, and I shared any words throughout this five-day fiasco. He said to me, "WTF is going on?" I didn't get a chance to respond before they marched us into separate cells. I was confused as to whether we had even been arrested as we were never Mirandized. I was too stunned to cry or even absorb what was happening. My vertigo kicked into high gear, and it was all I could do to focus. In fact, at one point, I fell off the wooden bench onto the floor. To which, a guard came in and plopped me back on the bench—no inquiry as to whether I was okay.

Once locked in jail, I was having a difficult time knowing I had no control over my fate. I saw the wall phone in the cell and made a gesture like I wanted to hang myself with the phone cord. Stupid, I know. While it is impossible to hang yourself by physically holding one end of the cord, law enforcement saw it another way. I was put on suicide watch which means I was to be treated lower than snail scum. Just me and a cold cement floor.

Because this all occurred Friday evening of President's Day weekend, the soonest we could get a bond hearing would be Tuesday morning. On Saturday morning, I was fingerprinted, and they took my mugshot. When a "prisoner" goes through intake, they are stripped down, ordered to bend over and cough. You can't appreciate how humiliating it is until you experience it. I was suited up in a grey and orange striped jumpsuit and given a pair of bright orange rubber flip flops sized Men XXL. After I was put on suicide watch, I received a black gunny sack style shift with Velcro attachments.

They then took me to another section of the jail where I got to share space with some other inmates. There were about a half dozen cells within a larger secure area; outside the cells was a picnic-style table, a TV, a shower, and a phone. I had a private cell as I was still on suicide watch. As you could potentially suffocate yourself with a mattress or pillow, I used three fat paperbacks as my pillow. My bed was a hard metal bunk, and the cold cement floor served as a seat. They gave me one thin blanket, and nothing else. No toothbrush, no soap, no cup, no basic necessities at all. They told me it was for my safety. Even if I had access to these items, what would I do with a toothbrush that has a two-inch handle to kill myself? A cup? Perhaps I could try to waterboard myself. And soap? Maybe jam it down my throat and choke. It would be easier to choke on the cold, rubbery hotdogs they served. No, it is not about safety and concern, it is deprivation and punishment. A subtle threat of "You're not checking out on my watch!"

I remained there for four more incredibly difficult and painful days. I repeatedly asked to talk to a sergeant or sheriff. I was not looking for special treatment, but they never gave me my one free phone call. My pleas fell on deaf ears. But then on Monday night, at 1 a.m., I finally was granted my phone call. I called my daughter, but she didn't pick up. Fortunately, she later saw it was a Louisiana number and called it, only to find out it was the county jail.

Still wrestling with the sudden loss of their father, my daughters, who live in the Midwest, were incredibly distraught that they could not reach Dean and me. They attempted to get more information once they figured out we were in the county jail, but their requests were denied.

On Monday, I was let out of my cell for thirty minutes to shower or make phone calls. As I was viewed as a suicide risk, everyone else had to go into their cells. I was so excited to be able to use the phone. However, the guard failed to inform me that you can only use the phone if you have money in your jail account, which of course, I did not. So, I wasted nearly the entire thirty minutes attempting to call people, but repeatedly, the calls would not go through. I was beyond frustrated.

On Tuesday morning, Dean and I were called to go in front of a judge via computer screen to receive our bail assessment. They set the bond at $16,000 for me and $5,000 for Dean. I thought we could now be released. However, I was so very wrong. I was taken back to the jail, still in lockdown, and on suicide watch. It turns out only the psychiatrist could release me, but he only came to the jail on Fridays. How could I get in a call to a bail bondsman if I could not access the phone? I had a bond set, I had the money to cover it, and I was still in jail! There was no such thing as innocent until proven guilty here. The prisoners who had been charged, tried, and found guilty had more privileges than Dean and I. The fact that Dean was even dragged into this mess still boggles my mind. He was only guilty by association of my poor judgment. We were never allowed to talk to one another and therefore could not develop a plan to get our sorry asses out of jail.

I had to wrap my head around spending another night or maybe many more in jail. At this point, I had no idea when I would be released. And then this happened: at about 1:00 a.m., a guard woke me up and told me to take my things (what things?) as I was being released. Through our kid's detective work, and my stepson having a credit card to pay our fees, they secured a bondsman (nearly impossible to do for those out of state), and Dean and I were going to be released.

Sharing this story with you takes courage. It would have been easier to sweep it under the rug and pretend it never happened. But what I've shared is all part of The Lemonade Legend movement I'm committed to promoting. My mission is to encourage people to be honest and real, and not hide behind a fake façade. As a result of this 61-year-old grandmother, business owner, and bearer of a squeaky-clean record, being naive and stubborn, I see the world differently. I now possess an arrest record of two misdemeanors and two felonies—all because of a taxi fare disagreement.

I share this story because never have I felt so helpless. In the midst of it, I realized I was being put to the test like never before. As the founder of Lemonade Legend, I wondered how I would make lemonade out of these lemons. The first two days, I beat myself up to the point where I was emotionally shattered. It occurred to me that if I genuinely wanted to commit suicide, as a human being, what I deserved was a little compassion and comfort. Ironically, being on suicide watch offered exactly the opposite. I realize now how it mirrors the pitifully broken mental health system in this country.

After two days, I transitioned into understanding and self-love. Through self-reflection, prayer, and meditation, I began to see my negative behavior with humility when feeling out of control. To survive this, I had to learn to be at peace with that. I gave it up to God, which allowed me to shed the anger, frustration, and anxiety like old useless skin. I completely surrendered and accepted my situation. I knew I had the strength to survive and the will to see it through. I channeled my good friend Holly Pasut, a contributor in The Lemonade Stand and author of A Strange Path to Freedom. I recalled the powerful insight she gave from being in federal prison for thirteen months. Throughout her ordeal, her takeaway was no one can control my mind. My thoughts remain mine, and I can choose my thoughts and focus on what is good, what is possible, and what place I mentally want to be in.

I had limited reading material, but an inmate shared a book by Matthew Kelly, founder of Dynamic Catholic. In it, he offered a spiritual explanation for hard times, in that God has a purpose and a mission for you; however, sometimes he needs to prepare you. That was a defining moment for me. I gained such clarity of the mission of Lemonade Legend. I experienced first-hand what it was like to not have a voice. I was in jail, I was not in control, and no one heard me as the person I was. It was no different than someone in an abusive relationship, being raped, trapped in a horrific job, or enmeshed in a cancer diagnosis.

No one should ever be forcibly silenced, shut out, and disregarded. Prisons do not have to be just physical. Some of us are locked in situational prisons. We all need a voice, to let go of the shame, and receive support. Lemonade Legend is all about helping people be heard.

As far as Dean and I, we are home in Arizona safe, and no longer felons. It was a long process due to Covid-19. Our trial date originally set for May 6 did not happen until July. With a voice of gratitude, I share that all charges were dismissed, and the District Attorney apologized to us for the way everything was handled. It may continue to follow us with some level of inconvenience because the arrest is still on our FBI reports. But God gave us his grace and patience to get through it and with forgiveness for less than perfect decisions.

On a side note, I learned Louisiana is influenced by Napoleonic law from their French roots. St. Bernard Parish has a harsh, extremely bad-ass law enforcement mentality. It is rare for a bail bondsman to take an out-of-town case. They are considered too much of a flight risk. If not for the guy that took pity on us, pulled a background check, and made a case with his boss to put up our bond, we might have been forced to stay in jail until our case was heard. Not only would this have caused severe injuries, if not death to my business, but also my health as I would not have been able to access my medication. I can only imagine what other trauma would have resulted.

Sometimes it takes a village, like our kids coming to the rescue, and in some situations, like our bail bondsman, it only takes one person to say, "I believe in you, you don't deserve this, and I'm here to help." Consider Lemonade Legend to be that for you.

About the Author

Michelle Faust is the founder of Lemonade legend, a company offering both print and media exposure through her anthology series, digital magazine, a publishing house, podcast, and virtual stages and two upcoming TV shows. Her ideal client is women (and a few brave men) who have lemonade stories to share and need a platform that shines the spotlight on them. The inception of The Lemonade Stand started with her own self-realization that she had a story herself of learning how to acquire a fearless attitude due to having a severe hearing loss which had impacted her own self-worth and created limiting beliefs. Her story is full of vulnerability, courage, and learning how to cope in a world which values perfection by developing her alternative strengths. After 20 years in the pharmaceutical industry, she elected to leap into the entrepreneurial world and follow her heart, which ultimately led to the creation of Lemonade Legend. Her book anthology, The Lemonade Stand, is her passion project that not only provides a powerful resource for women struggling with their own lemonade challenges but is also emerging into a community of like-minded women who want to share, support, and lift up their sisters.

Her mission is to create the largest storytelling distribution network in the world, to give people a voice, share their stories, and elevate them above the conventional noise. She connects people with their stories and their stories with the world. There is power in storytelling, and her platforms celebrate the voice of entrepreneurs and small business owners who have tackled lemons and created amazing versions of lemonade opportunities. Her network features individuals who have a powerful vision that is stronger than their fear. She provides extensive media exposure to brand their strength and courage.

Contact Information

www.lemonadelegend.com
hello@lemonadelegend.com
https://www.facebook.com/LemonadeLegend

AFTERWARD

At the time of this writing, I recently celebrated the one-year anniversary of the launch of "The Lemonade Stand" (Book 1). It feels more like a birthday than an anniversary, as it truly was a re-birth and changed the trajectory of my life forever.

My earliest work experience was volunteering at the local library. The librarians did not keep track of me and the time it took to re-shelve books so I would get lost in the aisles, surrounded by the smell of both old and newly pressed pages. I was filled with wonder at the abundance of stories about history, magic, drama, miracles, and marvelous follies. Rows of beautifully bound books like artisan craft to both my sight and touch.

I loved all kinds of books, but as I grew older, I found myself drawn to memoirs, historical fiction, true-life tales of adventure, journeys, and escapades. Nothing is more interesting or stranger than life itself. Fiction can be entertaining and a means of mental escape, but a scripted tale has a determined conclusion. Life has no guarantees, no signs to tell you which road to take, the outcome is revealed through the actions and behaviors of the main character. And that my friend is what inspires me and fills my soul with hope and sometimes tough lessons that need to be learned.

When "The Lemonade Stand" was released on December 4, 2019. It was the most glorious day of my life. The celebration, congratulations, accolades, and adrenaline pulsing through mt body was a day like no other. However, it is what happened in the year that followed that redefined my life goals and purpose. The bond created between myself and fellow authors of the book will forever be the greatest gift I have ever received. Second to that, was the encouragement to help others to share their stories.

Little did I, or anyone else know what was in store for 2020. Perhaps it is during our darkest times that we reach deep inside to challenge ourselves to get out of our comfort zone and see what we can do. If the world was falling apart what did I have to lose?

I continued to hear from my authors how healing the process of putting their stories down on paper was. I found myself in the middle of women who wanted to share their story but did not know how. I believe because of the hurt that 2020 brought to so many of us around the world, that it became more important than ever. If not to leave a legacy than to heal themselves, unleash the burden of unforgiveness, or to find their purpose in this world of uncertainty.

So, I set out to create the largest storytelling distribution network in the world. Quite an intimidating goal for me, but it felt right, it was my cloak of many colors that felt good to wear. It hugged my body in all the right places. God knows I needed hugs. In a years' time, Lemonade Legend has developed a publishing company, a digital magazine, spotlight magazine, a podcast, virtual events, and two TV shows to be aired on Zondra TV Network. None of this would have happened without an amazing tribe of supporters, coaches, mentors, and incredible connections.

And now we have unveiled "The Lemonade Stand" Book 2. Again, I have joined with 14 individuals of courage, determination, and inspiration. We share a bond that includes the authors of Book 1. It is like a special sorority of Lemonade Sisters and a brother. I am so honored to be trusted with their stories and most intimate feelings. I celebrate their commitment to unveil their authentic, beautiful, and raw selves to lift others and help us all to carry on in this strange new world. I am confident that each of these original stories have renewed your spirit and fed your soul with endless possibilities, of how you can be the architect of your own destiny.

Vickie Mudra shares her feelings here of being an author in Book 1. I encourage you to read it and think about how sharing your story can have a powerful impact on your life.

The Convergence of Self: Finding Your Purpose in Writing Your Story
– By Vickie Mudra

In early 2019, I was presented with an opportunity to participate in an anthology "The Lemonade Stand" By December of 2019, I could finally say I was a bestselling, published author. But I discovered that it was not the lovely, printed book that ended up being the greatest outcome for me. Instead, I found it was the action of stepping into and through the convergence of my various past and present self – child and adult, mother and daughter, wife, sister, friend, victim, survivor, nurturer, professional, leader, learner, teacher, and caregiver. The actual process of writing the story became the greatest gift I could ever have imagined. I started to refocus and reframe my childhood and my career and search for meaning in the events.

I began to see my purpose and passions unfold. Writing my story allowed me to gaze into the face of each age and each version of myself. I was able to ask who needed to be forgiven, who needed to be loved, who had something to teach me. During the writing process, I was able to connect with others who were on the same journey; eighteen other women who had full, rich lives that were not perfect, but were beautiful examples of bravery, life choice, resilience, and fortitude.

Made in the USA
Middletown, DE
17 March 2021

35341191R00159